A PRIEST FOREVER

A PRIEST FOREVER

NINE SIGNS OF RENEWAL AND HOPE

ALFRED McBRIDE,
O. PRAEM.

ST. ANTHONY MESSENGER PRESS
Cincinnati, Ohio

RESCRIPT

In accord with the *Code of Canon Law*, I hereby grant my permission to publish *A Priest Forever: Nine Signs of Renewal and Hope*, by Alfred McBride, O.PRAEM.

Most Reverend Carl K. Moeddel
Vicar General and Auxiliary Bishop
of the Archdiocese of Cincinnati
Cincinnati, Ohio
November 5, 2009

The permission to publish is a declaration that a book or pamphlet is considered to be free from doctrinal or moral error. It is not implied that those who have granted the permission to publish agree with the contents, opinions or statements expressed.

Scripture passages have been taken from *New Revised Standard Version Bible*, copyright ©1989 by the Division of Christian Education of the National Council of the Churches of Christ in the U.S.A., and used by permission. All rights reserved.

Cover and book design by Mark Sullivan
Cover image © Con Tanasiuk / Design Pics Inc./ gettyimages.com

LIBRARY OF CONGRESS CATALOGING-IN-PUBLICATION DATA
McBride, Alfred.
A priest forever : nine signs of renewal and hope / Alfred McBride.
p. cm.
ISBN 978-0-86716-954-6 (pbk. : alk. paper) 1. Priesthood—Catholic Church. 2. Pastoral theology—Catholic Church. I. Title.
BX1913.M37 2010
253—dc22

2009045555

ISBN 978-0-86716-954-6

Published by St. Anthony Messenger Press
28 W. Liberty St.
Cincinnati, OH 45202
www.SAMPBooks.org

Printed in the United States of America.

Printed on acid-free paper.

10 11 12 13 14   5 4 3 2 1

CONTENTS

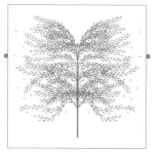

FEED MY PEOPLE

AMONG THE MANY APPEALING PRIESTS OF RECENT HISTORY WAS POPE JOHN XXIII. When a priest like him is unashamedly loved, folktales surround him. It is said that he found the papal slippers too soft to sustain his ample girth when he tried to walk in the gardens. When a local shoemaker provided a pair of sturdy red shoes for the Holy Father, workers at the Vatican pointed gleefully at the pope and said, "There goes Johnny Walker Red." Little stories like that capture the affection for priests—from our local parish to the majesty of St. Peter's—who know their role is to love God and people with all their hearts.

Was not Jesus trying to tell us this about the priesthood in that unforgettable scene by the shimmering waters of Lake Galilee? In the freshness of morning the apostles have brought in the latest catch of fish. Jesus cooked some fish over a fire and said, "Come, have breakfast." Then he served them bread and fried fish. When they had finished breakfast, Jesus discussed the ultimate meaning of priesthood by engaging Peter in a dialogue about love. You all know the story: Three times Jesus asks Peter, "Do you love me more than these?" Each time Peter says yes. Three times Jesus concludes each phase with the Great Commission, "Feed my people." Yes, I know he actually spoke of sheep and lambs, but he was really talking about people (see John 20:12–19).

Jesus was instructing all the apostles about the meaning of priesthood. When you read the passage, listen to Christ speaking to you, "Do you love me, Father?" Answer, "Yes Lord." Take to heart his Great Commission to you, "Feed my people." That simple dialogue is what this book is all about. These chapters briefly touch the ways you will love God and people as a priest. I ask you to look again at the quality of your relationship with Christ. I walk with you to the altar and the tabernacle and ask my brother priests with Saint Paul, "offer your bodies as a living sacrifice, holy and pleasing to God, your spiritual worship" (Romans 12:1).

I explore with you your commitment to feed our people and witness the church's social teachings. Pope Benedict's encyclical *Caritas in Veritate* refines that calling by asking us to have truth-drenched love in dealing with social issues. I will kneel with you as Jesus teaches us again how to pray. I think you will like my quotes on prayer from Cardinal Hume who said he needed to spend daily time in the desert if he expected to have something to say in the marketplace.

I invite you to find solutions to the crisis of priestly identity that plagues a number of the brothers. It's getting a lot better, but more help is on the way. I approach the lectern or pulpits with you to hear your homilies. I found Cardinal Levada's excellent lecture on preaching to be a treasure and I give you the source. I sit with you in the reconciliation room, both as a penitent and a confessor. I will wonder what you think of my emphasis on the priest as a man of personal mercy in all his dealings.

I go symbolically on pilgrimage to shrines of Mary, not just around the world but in front of the Mary shrine in your parish church. Mary has a special love for priests. Don't miss it. I see with you the screen of your computer and pray you will never press the button that assails your chaste celibacy. I trust my words on chaste living as a priest ring true for you. Finally, with the glorious Easter dawn in mind, I search the American landscape for fresh growth in vocations as well as new hope in the hearts of priests who again say "Yes, Lord" to the challenge to love God and our beloved people. I see in faith the resurrection of the American priesthood.

Yes, I think our Good Shepherd is bringing us back.

CHAPTER ONE

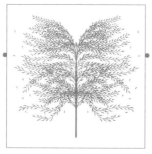

STAY CLOSE TO JESUS

"May nothing visible or invisible rob me of my prize, which is Jesus Christ."[1]

—*Saint Ignatius of Antioch*

IN 1987 I HAD THE GOOD FORTUNE TO REPRESENT ONE OF OUR BISHOPS to the media during Pope John Paul II's second pastoral visit to the United States. My main duty was to answer questions posed by reporters. I spent most of my time in large hotel halls set aside for the media.

Much of what I saw of the pope was on TV, though I also attended one function each day to watch the Holy Father in action. This pope felt a deep responsibility for the pastoral care of priests as evidenced by his annual Holy Thursday letter to priests. In each of the nine cities he visited, his first meeting was usually with priests, as the following story illustrates.

Pope John Paul II began his visit at Miami's St. Mary's Cathedral. Priests from all over the country filled the church. After the scriptural prayer service, Father Francis McNulty delivered an address to our Holy Father on behalf of American priests. He opened with a familiar anecdote:

> A lavish dinner to honor a visiting actor concluded with the host asking the actor to deliver some of his favorite lines. The actor recited a sonnet from Shakespeare, "Shall I compare thee to a summer's day?" and the opening soliloquy from Richard III, "Now is the winter of our discontent..." to much applause. The host then requested that he recite psalm 23. The speaker said, "I will be happy to do this if my priest friend, seated next to me, will also do this after I am finished." The priest agreed.
>
> The guests applauded the actor's dramatic rendering of that beautiful psalm. Then the priest arose and spoke the words as a prayer, in so personal a tone that it seemed as though the words were flowing straight from his heart to the hearts of the listeners. The listeners greeted Father's recital with deep silence.
>
> The actor stood up and said, "Do you realize what just happened? You applauded my delivery. You responded to the priest with quiet silence. What did this mean? It revealed that I knew the Shepherd Psalm, but that Father knew the Shepherd."

By starting his talk before the pope with this touching anecdote, the gifted Father McNulty set a tone of faith and drew the attention of all priests to their primary goal, namely, to know, love, and identify with the real Good Shepherd, Jesus Christ.

A few years ago I came across a news item about a priest in Philadelphia, of interest to me as I was born and raised in the city of brotherly love. Father Francis Giliberti, pastor of a poor parish, St. Barbara's, regularly met with his parish council. On one occasion he noted a twenty thousand dollar debt from the renovation of the parish hall. He told his council that he didn't know where the money would come from, but that God would find a way. It just so happened he was going to spend his day off in Atlantic City. At a slot machine in one of the casinos he hit the jackpot. The prize was a million dollars.

The next time he met with the parish council, he told them not to worry about the debt on the hall. When interviewed by the local press he was asked what he was going to do with the money. How would he spend it? On himself? He replied. "I don't need the money. I have all I ever wanted or needed in being a priest. My priesthood is my treasure. I have Jesus as my best friend." He went on to say he would give the money to a scholarship fund for poor students to help them attend Catholic high schools in Philadelphia. Father Giliberti knew the Good Shepherd. (Please do not take this story as approval of gambling to solve church debts!)

For nine years I taught seminarians at Blessed John XXIII Seminary in Weston, Massachusetts. Cardinal Cushing founded the seminary for older men. Cushing believed that Christ called older men to the priesthood. He was not facing a priest shortage in those days, but encountering a spiritual reality and creating a concrete response. The age range for the seminarians during my years there was generally thirty-five to fifty, with some exceptions. The enrollment held steady at seventy-two men and continues as such today.

Many of my students were widowers with children and grandchildren. One man I remember was George Wilkinson. He and his wife raised eleven children. He was a Washington, D.C., lawyer who did a fair amount of pro-bono practice. My main teaching duty was training the men in preaching. I encouraged them to begin each talk with a story as an icebreaker for the listeners. One tale George told us concerned a conversation with his wife. It went like this: "Mary, would you die for me?" She said, "No. I would die to defend our children. I would die to stand up for my faith. But for you, George, I want to live." Time seemed to stop for a moment for all of us when we heard her testament of love and to know she loved him to the end.

A year after George was ordained he sent us a letter that reminded me how elated an older man should be with his priesthood:

> I am still on an ebullient high. There has to be a time when it subsides. I hope not for years. To be God's servant for the purpose of loving his people can only be experienced, and then to be paid in addition! Priesthood has to be the best-kept secret in the world. I wonder how I could be so blessed.... Confessions are at least as important to me as to the penitent. To be able to give God's pardon and his peace of mind and heart seems to me little short of a miracle.[2]

George's thoughts are not atypical among our seminary alumni. I used to think that first fervor was the property of the young, something I experienced in spades. But to see God's grace being just as soul-stirring in men in the autumn of their lives is in many ways more inspiring.

In the 1970s I worked at the National Catholic Education Association (NCEA). I was the staff member for religious education, meaning I was called to help improve the state of teaching religion in the Catholic schools and in the parish programs for students in public education. It was a challenging duty but also very satisfying. I traveled, on average, to thirty cities a year, conducting seminars or giving talks at diocesan workshops on religious education. I also ran the program for these matters at our annual convention.

One year we held our convention In New York City. Our cast of speakers was more celebrated due to the setting. I recall Henri Nouwen speaking to three thousand people in St. Patrick Cathedral. His talk drew from his excellent work on the Prodigal Son and the need to be a wounded healer. We also were honored to have Mother Teresa and Archbishop Camara as copresenters in one session. The nun and the priest were outstanding servants of the poor of the world.

Teresa's mission was better known and her message was that great works were not needed; everyday duties done with great love will save the world. But Camara's reputation for upholding the "preferential option for the poor" in Brazil was just getting to be widely known and appreciated. To see these two icons of holiness and social concern on the same stage was enough to fill any Catholic or person of goodwill with hope for our future.

• •

BORN TO BE A PRIEST

Being a priest isn't just a choice; it's a way of life. It's what water is for a fish, the sky for a bird. I really believe in Christ. Jesus for me is not an abstract idea—he's a personal friend.

Being a priest has never disappointed me.... Celibacy, chastity, the absence of a family...all this has never been a burden to me.... If you only knew what I feel when I say Mass, how I become one with it! The Mass for me is truly Calvary, and the Resurrection: it's a mad joy!

Look, there are those born to sing, those who are born to write, those who are born to play soccer.... I was born to be a priest...not because my parents put the idea in my head. My father was a Mason, and my mother went to Church once a year.

I even remember that one day my father got frightened and said: "My son. You are always saying you want to be a priest. But do you know what that means? A priest is someone who doesn't belong to himself, because he belongs to God and to his people..."

And I said, "I know. That's why I want to be a priest."[3]

• •

The connection between the priesthood and Christ is the theme of this chapter. The above stories are my attempt to put flesh and blood on this aspect of the priest's life. During the year of Saint Paul there was renewed attention given to the richness of his teachings on a number of topics. I have always been attracted to his incredible unity with Christ. Considering he once wanted to kill people who loved Jesus and stamp out Christianity before it got started— and then wound up saying, "For me to live is Christ" is astonishing. My following reflection is meant to cause a fresh awareness of Paul's profound relationship with Jesus as a model for a priest's ultimate fulfillment.

I Live by Faith in the Son of God

Saint Paul's conversion began with a profound religious experience of Jesus Christ, our Risen Lord and Savior. Saint Paul used the expression "in Christ" 165 times in his writings, most frequently with the title "Kyrios" or "Lord." Paul is saturated with Christ Jesus. He spent over seven years of solitude and prayer growing in union with Christ. No wonder he could say with immense conviction:

> For I am convinced that neither death nor life, nor angels, nor principalities, nor present things, nor future things, nor powers, nor height, nor depth, nor any other creature will be able to sep- arate us from the love of God in Christ Jesus our Lord. (Romans 8:37–39)

The church is the body of Christ. The head Christ and the members of the body belong together. We may not say, I love Christ but I do not need the church. Saint Paul would respond immediately, "We, though many, are one body in Christ, and individually parts of one another" (Romans 12:5).

Those who want a Christian spirituality without the church miss the teachings of Paul. "God gave Christ as head over all things to the church, which is his body" (Ephesians 1:22–23). To want the head without the body is to contradict Christ's purpose for us.

At his best the priest is a link between the head and the members of the Body of Christ. The priest is a churchman, a minister ordained to serve the members, the people of God. This is most evident when the priest celebrates the Eucharist and, as an instrument of the Holy Spirit, brings the bread to be Christ's Body and the wine to be Christ's Blood to the faithful for their salvation and closer union with Jesus. The priest is a bridge between the head Christ and the members, God's people. We call the pope a *pontiff* which is a Latin word meaning "to build a bridge." The pope is *pontiff maximus*, or the maximum bridge-builder for the church, but every priest has this calling. Of course none of this is possible without union with Christ and his empowering graces.

Columba Marmion's Passion for Christ

When I was a seminarian I was shaped by the writings of Dom Columba Marmion. He was born and raised in Dublin and eventually entered the seminary. For his theological studies he was sent to Rome. There he came under the influence of Benedictine liturgical scholars. He developed a longing to join their order. After his ordination he confided his desires to his Irish bishop, who decided that this young priest should spend five years serving in Dublin's parishes. If his perceived vocation to the Benedictines survived, then he would be released for this calling.

The young Columba persisted and the bishop finally released him. Marmion moved to Belgium and joined the monks of Maredsous. Slowly he made his way among his brethren. He was recruited as a teacher and for other responsibilities. Eventually, he was elected abbot. His reputation as a spiritual guide grew. His conferences were so compelling that one of the monks made shorthand copies that became the sources of his books.

His spirituality was grounded in Scripture, centered on Christ, and heavily influenced by Saint Paul. Marmion emphasized that the result of being a member of Christ's body is a participation in the life of God. We are adopted children of God. What Jesus is by nature, we are by the grace of adoption. Marmion loved Saint Paul's powerful opening to his letter to the Ephesians: "Blessed be the God and Father of our Lord Jesus Christ who has blessed us in Christ with every spiritual blessing.... In love he destined us for adoption to himself through Jesus Christ" (Ephesians 1:3, 5).

Blessed Abbot Marmion dwelt on that verse with prayer and faith for many years. He was inspired to write four spiritual classics based on that text: *Christ, the Life of the Soul, Christ the Ideal of the Monk, Christ in His Mysteries, Christ: The Ideal of the Priest*. Like a modern Saint Paul he reclaimed the power of Christ for the contemporary church and for the proper understanding of church as Christ's saving presence in the world. Marmion showed us again that Christ's salvation was a matter of deliverance from sin, but also a resurrection to new life, a participation in the life of God. Marmion encourages us to renew our faith in this truth about ourselves, whether we are the lay faithful, priests, or religious. His books drew their power from the same insight as he wrote:

> Oh, if we had faith in these truths! If we understood what it is for
> us to have entered by Baptism into the Church, to be by grace,

members of Christ's body! Join Saint Augustine who says, "Let us break forth into thanksgiving. Let us wonder and thrill with gladness; we are become Christ. He the head, we the members."[4]

When I lived in Belgium in 1963 attending courses at Lumen Vitae, I made pilgrimage to Maredsous Abbey to visit the tomb of Abbot Marmion. In those days his body was stored in the vault of the abbots underneath the church. His casket was on a shelf along with others. A lone kneeler was placed before it. It seemed a dusty, unworthy place for someone who meant so much to me.

But in October of the year 2000, along with thirty others from Boston, I was in Rome for the beatification of Pope John XXIII. Providentially, Abbot Marmion was also being beatified in the presence of thousands in St. Peter's Square. Back at his abbey, his body—no longer stored in a vault—was now buried in the abbey church and a center of veneration for many and, God willing, remaining there until the Resurrection. Of course, Blessed Columba had already gone to glory. His writings continued to motivate many seminarians, priests, and lay faithful to become aware of their dignity as adopted children of God, participating in Christ's own life.

The Name of Jesus: A Clap of Thunder

Throughout the years I have been spiritually nourished by the Office of Readings in the Liturgy of the Hours. This prayer book of the church is in a special way the ordinary prayer of priests. I tend to keep a pen available to underline passages that appeal to me, to make notes in the margins and to keep a record of the page numbers in the opening and closing pages of the four volumes. I am often drawn by the Holy Spirit to pay closer attention to phrases and sentences that illuminate my relationship with Christ.

Such is the reading for May 20, when we celebrate the memorial of Saint Bernardine of Siena (1380–1444) who was a fiery preacher in the style of Saint Paul. He attributed his effectiveness to his emphasis on the name of Jesus:

> The name of Jesus is the glory of preachers, because the shining splendor of that name causes his word to be proclaimed and heard.… When a fire is lit to clear a field, it burns off all the dry and useless weeds and thorns. When the sun rises and darkness is dispelled, robbers, night-prowlers and burglars hide away. So when Paul's voice was raised to preach the Gospel to the nations, like a great clap of thunder in the sky, his preaching was a blazing fire carrying all before it.[5]

This passage also compels my attention when I think of the pervasive, irreverent misuse of Christ's name in novels, films, and everyday conversation. It makes me think of Saint Bernadine's passionate love for Jesus and his name. As a priest ordained to be another Christ in the world, I am reminded of my need to help people recover a respect for Jesus' name by developing a loving relationship with him, even as I must do so myself.

An Explosion of Insights About Jesus

In this same spirit Paul enshrines two of the most exalted hymns of the early church: In Philippians 2:1–11, Paul presents us with the divine humility of Christ, who empties himself of glory and dies for our salvation. "Therefore, God bestowed on him a name that is above every other name." A popular hymn captures this: "Every knee shall bow, every tongue confess that Jesus Christ is Lord."

In Colossians 1:15–20 Paul portrays Jesus as the wisdom of God—as the one in whom all was created and who made peace by the blood of the cross. "For in him all the fullness was pleased to dwell, and through him to reconcile all things for him." Paul tells us that authentic faith in Christ means belonging to his body, the church.

It is likely these two hymns were written before Paul's conversion, but used by him to great effect when appreciating the extraordinary role of Christ in our lives. Pope Benedict XVI has pondered the remarkable development of language to express the meaning of Jesus in the twenty years after his Resurrection and Ascension into heaven. Benedict thinks of this as an "explosion" of incomparable insights which Paul preserved and the church sings every week of the liturgical year.

Pope Benedict puts it this way: "How could these unknown groups be so creative? How were they so persuasive...? Isn't it more logical, even historically speaking, to assume that the greatness came at the beginning, and that the figure of Jesus really did explode all existing categories and could only be understood in the light of the mystery of God?"[6]

The theological depths of the Philippians hymn celebrating the divine humility of Jesus and the Colossians hymn to Jesus as divine wisdom signal a breathtaking cataract of faith in the earliest days of the church. The ordained priesthood and the priesthood of all the faithful alike were seized by the Holy Spirit in an *explosion* of intuitive appreciation of who was this Jesus with whom they have a fruitful relationship.

The first step in our celebration of ordained priesthood is to reflect on our friendship with Jesus. No priest worthy of the name can hope to be a blessing to God's people without a loving, prayerful, and insightful relationship with Jesus Christ, the Son of God and the Son of Mary.

For Reflection

1. What is the state of my relationship with Jesus?
2. Who are my role models for spiritual growth?
3. How do I renew my enthusiasm for priesthood?
4. When do I take time to grow in love of Christ and my people?
5. How do I function as a bridge between God and my parish?

● ●

"My God, if my tongue cannot say in every moment that I love You, I want my heart to repeat it to You as often as I draw breath."[7]

—*Saint John Vianney, Cure of Ars*

CHAPTER TWO

THE EUCHARIST

Share with all the word of God you have received with joy. Believe what you read. Teach what you believe. Practice what you teach.[1]

—*Rite of Ordination*

ONE OF THE SPECIAL PLEASURES I ENJOYED DURING MY YEARS AT BLESSED John XXIII Seminary was weekend Masses at Sacred Heart Parish in Quincy, Massachusetts. Settled in that historic town, the church was but a few blocks from the home of John Adams, our second president. The rectory was the home of a priest's priest, Father Neil Heery. Just after Christmas, on Saint Patrick's Day, and on other occasions his rectory was open house for dozens of priests to come and socialize.

His associates over the years marveled at his attention to them. Father Daniel O'Connell recalled Neil saying, "Daniel, come and say a prayer with me." Daniel recalled that, "At the end of my long days he waited up to hear my adventures and misadventures. He'd say, 'How did things go? Were there many people? What did you say?' Father Heery would make a connection between me and him. He'd then go on to remind me of my connection with God."

The axiom "No priest without the Eucharist, no Eucharist without the priest," was engraved in Father Heery's heart. His devotion to the Mass was admirable. He loved adoration of the Blessed Sacrament and instituted daily exposition of the Sacrament in the Mass chapel from nine to five, Monday through Friday. He saved his time for adoration from four-thirty to five. At the time I knew him best there were four young men from the parish in the seminary. All were ordained and, thank God, remain in ministry.

On a frosty night after Christmas 1995, Father Heery received a sick call. The parishioner lived on the third floor of a three-storey apartment building. As Neil walked up the stairs he suffered agonizing chest pains. He continued with his priestly work, anointed the woman, comforted her briefly, and went home. Feeling severely ill, he asked the associate to drive him to the hospital where he was admitted to intensive care—he had had a heart attack. Fifty priests tried to visit him, but he was too ill to receive company. After forty-five years as a priest, he died on January 12, 1996. For his funeral, Cardinal Law and three hundred priests—plus a church packed upstairs and down—attended. Six football players from the local public high school served as pallbearers. Neil was a reliable fan of their team.

Father James Hawker, who lived with Father Neil for twenty years at Sacred Heart, wrote,

You don't know a person until you live with him.

How often, as many are aware, Neil repeated one or another of three short sentences. They captured succinctly his view of life and reality.

"We have been blessed beyond measure." …He was so grateful to God for the many people whom he met along the way. Whether family or friend, priest or parishioner, Neil knew that each contributed uniquely to the fabric of his life.

"You have given of your treasure." He believed that the vibrancy and vitality of a parish could not be measured simply in dollars and cents…. Neil was much more comfortable when speaking on behalf of the St. Vincent de Paul Society [than for the grand annual collection.] He reserved a special place in his heart for the elderly who "had borne the heat of the day."

"Having said that, I'll say no more." Each afternoon at three o'clock the crowd would convene and discuss informally endless issues of mutual interest. Always the respectful listener, Neil would consider patiently the ideas and opinions that were bandied about…. With an economy of words he so often conveyed a wealth of wisdom. In having said the least he shared the most…. As he ascended the stairs he would often repeat once again, "Having said that, I'll say no more."[2]

The Priest Offers Christ and Himself at Mass

"Those who belong to Christ have crucified their flesh with its passions and desires."—Galatians 5:24

"I have been crucified with Christ."—Galatians 2:19

Prior to Christ, the Levitical priests offered sacrifices of lambs and bulls—substitutes for themselves. But Jesus, our High Priest on the cross, gave himself to the Father for our salvation. He was the real Lamb of God. In Mozart's heart-melting music for the *Ave Verum* we hear that Jesus is truly born of Mary (*vere natum*) and truly sacrificed (*vere immolatum*). At the first Eucharist Jesus offered his body "to be given up" for us and sacrificed his blood which "will be shed that sins may be forgiven."

Archbishop Fulton Sheen, in his powerful book on the priest-hood, explores this theme at great length:

> Do we offer at Mass as if we presented a victim for sin who was totally unrelated to us, like the scapegoat or the bird? ...Do we offer the Christ-Savior to the Father as if we were not dying with Him?
>
> We cannot escape reproducing in our souls the mystery enacted on the altar.... As our Lord immolated Himself, so do we immolate ourselves....
>
> Shall we eat bread and give no wheat to be ground? Shall we drink wine and give no grapes to be crushed? The condition for incorporation into the Resurrection and Ascension of Christ and into His glorification is incorporation into His death."[3]

Saint Paul opens the twelfth chapter of his letter to the Romans precisely with this reality of living the Eucharist. "I urge you, therefore, brothers, by the mercies of God, to offer your bodies as a living sacrifice, holy and pleasing to God, your spiritual worship" (Romans 12:1). Should not all our brothers in the priesthood gather these words into their hearts as they begin each Mass? Is there not great value in approaching the sacrifice of Christ with these words stirring us to be committed to sacrificial love in our lives? What greater way is there for priests to raise the host and the chalice than to have the attitude that consecrates our bodies as a living sacrifice to the Lord?

One of the beautiful outcomes of the Vatican Council was a renewal of our appreciation of Christ's resurrection in our salvation. The faith of the church in Easter was never lost, but somehow was overshadowed by the cross. However, it is typically human to go to extremes. Suddenly, it was all Easter and not much cross. Why do we tend to close a door when we open a window?

I remember one experience in that period when I was to give a presentation at a religious education congress. When I arrived I saw all the participants wearing large yellow buttons on which were printed the words "I am an alleluia from head to toe." Behind the lettering was a vague image of Christ rising from the dead. Now, this verse is certainly true. But in a culture that is pleasure addicted and which causes people to think they have a right not to suffer, this becomes an exaggeration that abandons the role of the cross in salvation and at Mass.

When Saint Paul arrived in Corinth he encountered an easygoing culture that lived by the motto, "Pleasure is the measure of being human." I don't mean to be a killjoy, but real "reality shows" would always have tragedies and sorrows embedded in the act of pleasure. Just as in Corinth, is not the cross today a stumbling block?

At that congress I commented on the beautiful buttons and challenged the listeners to remember Saint Paul confronting the Corinthians.

We proclaim Christ crucified, stumbling block to Jews and foolishness to gentiles, but to those who are called, Jews and Greeks alike, Christ the power and wisdom of God…When I came to you, brothers, proclaiming the mystery of God, I did not come with sublimity of wisdom. For I resolved to know nothing while I was with you except Jesus Christ, and him crucified. (1 Corinthians 2:23–24; 1–2)

Vocations

For years now bishops and religious superiors have struggled with the catastrophe of a perilous drop in vocations. In the United States we have more Catholics than ever and need more priests than ever to serve them. There is a noticeable increase of vocations for the diocesan priesthood, but, with few exceptions, our religious communities are not doing well, as of this writing. Pope John Paul has offered a fourfold plan for training seminarians that deals with their human development, spiritual growth, theological education, and pastoral skills. But in many instances the recruitment is weak and the application of the pope's agenda is uneven. In this regard I think Sheen's emphasis is worth remembering:

> Could it be that one reason for the lack of vocations is our failure to stress sacrifice? The young…want a mission, a challenge! When we follow the type of advertising appeal used by Madison Avenue to sell toothpaste, when we use commercial techniques in our vocation literature, do not the hearts of the young spurn our distance from the Cross? Do we not recruit fruits of propaganda rather than fruits worthy of penance?[4]

I have observed that the dioceses which have growing numbers of vocations are the result of bishops who take an active role in seeking recruits. The new archbishop of Saint Louis, Robert Carlson, is a veritable pied piper of vocations. He and others take a challenging approach to vocations, not offering an easy life but one that is demanding and not for the faint of heart. Allied to any successful recruiting of vocations is the need for seminaries that are not soft on formation.

The passion of Christ was not an easy road. The cross was daunting. Why should seminarians be deluded in thinking that the priesthood has nothing to do with the hardships of Christ's life, passion, and death? Could it be that we priests and seminarians cannot honestly say with Saint Paul, "I have been crucified with Christ; yet I live, nor longer I, but Christ lives in me" (Galatians 2:19–20)? Every Sunday is an Easter for us. On the weekdays we endure the slings and arrows of outrageous fortune. We walk in the shadow of the cross and are purified by the Holy Spirit. American priests still receive a lot of respect due both to our struggle to be disciples of Christ and our lifelong service to God's people.

• •

MANY ALTARS, ONE FAITH

I have been able to celebrate Mass in chapels built along mountain paths, on lake shores and seacoasts; I have celebrated it on altars built in stadiums and in city squares…This varied scenario of celebrations of the Eucharist has given me a powerful experience of its universal and so to speak, cosmic character. Yes cosmic!

Because even when it is celebrated on the humble altar of a country church, the Eucharist is always in some way celebrated on the altar of the world. It unites heaven and earth. It embraces and permeates all creation (Ecclesia de Eucharistia, 8).

> Know that in this bread is the body of Christ
> which hung on the cross,
> and in this cup, the blood of Christ
> which flowed from his side.
> Take, therefore, and eat his body;
> take and drink his blood,
> and you will become members of his body.
> Eat this sacred food,
> so that your bond of unity with Christ may never be broken.
> Drink this sacred blood, the price he paid for you,
> so that you may never lose heart because of your sinfulness.[5]

• •

Lift Up Your Heart: Francis Xavier Van Thuan

While in Rome for the beatification of Pope John XXIII, our pilgrimage group assembled for dinner at a garden restaurant on our last night. Our honored guest was Archbishop Francis Xavier Van Thuan. His after-dinner talk dealt with his imprisonment and devotion to the Mass.

> I was in Saigon the week that the Americans left my country. Planes and copters were hauling your troops by the thousands to ships offshore headed for America. Many of my people who had helped you vainly tried to get aboard and away. There was little room and the rush to escape was destined for your countrymen. I still see the tears and the dust and hear the cries.

A month later I was appointed bishop of Saigon. Barely had I begun my service than the government began to pressure me. I was to instruct my clergy that they may not preach against government policies. The authorities severely limited us from charitable care for our parishioners. The state will take care of everything. They wanted to interfere in the training of seminarians and reduced the number we could recruit. All this was accompanied by angry threats.

I refused to obey them. Within three months, they removed me from office, arrested me and put me in prison where I lived for the next thirteen years. The last half of that imprisonment I was in solitary confinement. There I was in a dark cell with no one to talk to other than the six guards, two every eight hours. They were forbidden to converse with me. I knew that I loved God and could continue to do so in jail. My inner life was free.

But I also concluded that I have a calling to love my enemies. So I set out to show my guards that I loved them. It wasn't easy. But gradually I found ways to show my interest in their needs. I asked them about their children, how many, their names, their ages, their health. I showed concern for their wives and parents and, gradually, the burdens of their lives both at the prison and in their neighborhoods. Somehow I was able to establish a relationship with them.

After many months I summoned the courage to ask them for a favor. Could they give me a piece of wood, some wire and—and holding my breath—a knife which they allowed me to keep for a few days. Many days passed, but finally they gave me what I requested. Secretly, I carved a cross with the knife and cut my bar of soap in half inside of which I hid the cross. Lastly, I twisted the

23

wire into a small chain. I now possessed again the cross and chain of a bishop. I never wore it visibly until my release years later. I am wearing that gift from God here tonight. By the way, I returned the knife.

I continued to foster the relationship with the guards. There were some changes and I had to start over with a new crew of hostile men. Eventually, I made a request. Could I have some bread and wine? My relatives would supply it. So much time passed that I believed they would not help me. Praise God, they arrived one day with a very small bit of wine and bread.

So began my Holy Thursdays and Corpus Christis and Easter Sundays to brighten up my daily Good Fridays. Each day I placed a tiny piece of bread and a few drops of wine in the palm of my hand and celebrated Mass. I had no beautiful vestments, no candlelight, no polished gold chalice, no lectionary, no sacramentary, no ordo, no altar, no choir or servers, no visible congregation. In faith, of course, I knew the Holy Trinity, the angels and saints and the Body of Christ on earth joined me in my cell, lent me their courage and I offered the Eucharist to praise God and help all people to receive salvation.

By the grace of God I was finally let free. Today I work with the Vatican's Office for justice and peace. They like to send me to minister to those who do not like each other. My prison training in loving my enemies is now finding a new audience.[6]

Archbishop Van Thuan was made a cardinal soon after this talk and died two years later. His struggle to have daily Mass in tough circumstances is a credit to his priesthood and a witness to all priests today to cherish the Eucharist with continued fidelity and love.

Two Priesthoods

In coming to the conclusion of this chapter, it is worth taking a little time to distinguish the ordained priesthood from the priesthood of all the faithful. During the Reformation Martin Luther downplayed the importance of ordained priests and elevated the priesthood of all the faithful. In reaction we stressed the ordination of the priest in holy orders and did not pay much attention to the common priesthood of all who have been baptized. That has been corrected by the catechesis of the sacraments and the document on the liturgy from Vatican II.

The precious gift of ordained or ministerial priesthood is given to the church in the sacrament of holy orders. Baptism initiates each member of the church into the common priesthood of all believers. The sacrament of holy orders confers special gifts on the ordained. Priests and bishops are celebrants of the Eucharist, reconciliation, and anointing. Only the bishop ordains priests and deacons. Only bishops ordain other bishops.

The two priesthoods differ but complement and enrich each other. "Though they differ essentially and not only in degree, the priesthood of the faithful and the ministerial priesthood are ordered to one another" (*Lumen Gentium,* 10). Christ calls all the baptized to share in the Spirit's work of sanctifying the world. Christ calls ordained priests to share in the Spirit's work of unfolding the baptismal graces of the faithful. Both forms of priesthood flow from Christ and are meant to carry his priestly mission to the world. The ordained and common priesthood enrich each other more fruitfully when coordinated for the common good of the Body of Christ.

I close this chapter with a quotation from Saint John Chrysostom's classical book on the ordained priesthood:

> When you behold the Lord immolated and lying on the altar, and the priest standing over the sacrifice and praying, and all the people purpled by that precious blood, do you imagine you are still on earth among men, and not rather rapt in heaven; and casting away all worldly thoughts from your mind, do you not contemplate with a clean heart and pure mind the things of heaven? O miracle! O goodness of God! He that sits above with the Father, is at that moment in the hands of all...and gives Himself to all who desire to embrace and receive Him. At that moment all do this with the eyes of faith.
>
> If you consider what it is for a man yet clothed in flesh and blood to approach that pure and blessed nature, you will easily understand to what a dignity the grace of the Holy Spirit has raised priests.[7]

For Reflection

1. How can we link ordained priesthood with baptismal priesthood?
2. Share some success stories about priests forming community.
3. How does the Eucharist help us be a faith community?
4. Who have you met that you would say is a priests' priest?
5. What do you admire in the way priests celebrate Mass?

• •

"Lord, grant me the conversion of my parish: I am willing to suffer whatever you wish, for my entire life!"[8]

—*Saint John Vianney*

CHAPTER THREE

THE CHURCH'S SOCIAL TEACHINGS

NORBERTINE FATHER ROBERT CORNELL WAS ONE OF THE TWO ELECTED priests in the House of Representatives toward the end of the twentieth century, the other being Jesuit Father Robert Drinan. Both were Democrats.

Father Cornell was a priest, an educator, and an elected official. I knew him well in all three roles. He was my homeroom teacher when I was a sophomore at Philadelphia's Southeast Catholic High School. Besides teaching five classes a day, he was finishing his theology courses after school to prepare for the priesthood.

In my junior year he was my American history teacher. From him I learned a lot about our presidents, wars, and development as a nation. I marveled at his capacity to lecture one hour for every class, rarely consulting notes. Later, he was famous for this skill throughout his forty years of teaching at St. Norbert College in De Pere,

Wisconsin. At the end of that year I took a train ride to Archmere Academy in Delaware to attend his ordination.

As a senior, I took his course on national problems. I received my first hints of his passion for the labor movement, and the needs of the working class and others who needed a public voice. His interest in the church's social teachings was already evident. Later his doctoral dissertation on the anthracite coal strike both echoed his social conscience and remains one of few among thousands of dissertations that is still read. (For example, mine isn't.)

I became one of his numerous lifelong friends after being in his classes five hours a week for forty weeks each of those three years. He was never an aloof teacher. He was interested in us as people. He had high standards, a great sense of humor, and devotion to us. Five of our senior class entered the Norbertines that year. All became priests permanently. Father Bob came to the B & O train station to see us off on our trip to De Pere and cheer us up.

Father Cornell's weekdays were devoted to teaching, but on weekends he served in local parishes such as Corpus Christi in Sturgeon Bay. It was there he conceived the idea of running concerts to make money for the parish. Later he moved the concerts to Green Bay, where the profits were donated for scholarships to Premontre High School and St. Norbert College. One of his favorite performers was Johnny Cash.

The year he was elected to his first term in congress (1975), I was a staff member at the National Catholic Educational Association on Dupont Circle in Washington, D.C. He lived with me that first year then moved to Capitol Hill for the convenience. I witnessed his growth as a member of Congress. People often asked him why a priest would want to be a politician. In his memoir he gave the answer, explaining that in May 1961, he gave a talk to an assembly of Catholic leaders on the church's social teachings as an answer to communism. The reception was cool. He had heard that one of his critics said, "Where does Cornell get all those crazy ideas?" He decided that talking about the church's social teachings was not enough. He believed that only by advocating social public policy in elective office was there hope of making needed social changes.

As a congressman he did exactly that. He always wore his priest collar and black clerical suit. He saw no conflict between his priesthood and political service. The National Right to Life organization gave him a 100 percent approval rating. He was an outstanding pro-life Democrat. In his last campaign he was compelled to abandon elective office by church authority. Yet he continued his defense of the poor, the working class, the needs of Vietnam veterans, family farms, local dairy farms—basically the underdogs of this world who need a voice. He did this through his monthly newspaper columns and letters to the editor and, in a deeper fashion, through his history classes at St. Norbert's.

A number of his students became his disciples, taking his ideals into careers as lawyers and teachers. One of his students, Brian Mathu, captured the magic of Father Bob's influence:

> Father Cornell will likely be remembered for his days in congress when he shook hands with presidents and worked with many influential people. But I will always picture him humbly talking with and listening to my young sons, giving them some loose change or a small toy as a gift and making them feel like the most important people in the world.

Father Bob was a star of our Norbertine community, but he never flaunted his celebrity among us. He returned to our community for the last twenty-nine years of his life. He was funny, passionate, and, yes, loving. This is why he attracted so many friends, and kept them, as Shakespeare wrote, "with hoops of steel."

In my countless conversations with him he would often break out with a little poem. He did not know the authors. It was like his confession of faith.

> To meet in heaven, how sweet the thought,
> When life's short years are past.
> No more to weep, no more to part,
> To meet in heaven at last.
> To meet in heaven around the throne
> Of him who died to save.
> Be this our hope, our anxious care,
> To meet beyond the grave.[1]

Preaching and Witnessing the Just Word

For over a century our popes have been active in developing the church's social teachings in the light of problems caused by the industrial and technological revolutions. Pope John XXIII taught that peace will come more easily when people are treated justly. Pope Paul VI argued that the rich nations of the world have a responsibility to help the poor ones.

Pope John Paul II has said that the state has an essential obligation to assure that workers can enjoy the fruits of their labors. While the state has an obligation to protect human rights in the economic sector, the responsibility for this is shared by churches, humanitarian associations, and similar institutions.

Fathers Cornell and Drinan tried to do this in the political realm, but many other priests continue this mission in their classrooms, pulpits, and parish programs. A powerful example may be found in the program Preaching the Just Word, implemented by Father Raymond Kemp of the Washington archdiocese and the late Jesuit Walter Burghardt. Sponsored by the Woodstock Theological Center, they brought the church's social teachings to parishes, seminaries, colleges, and other organizations throughout our country.

Preaching the Just Word opens the Scriptures and brings out the rich teachings of social justice inaugurated by the prophets, especially Amos and Isaiah, and fulfilled in the vision of the kingdom of God, preached and witnessed by Jesus as a kingdom of love, justice, and mercy.

Attention to the message of Amos, as Israel's first reforming prophet, centers on his teaching that God is the Lord of justice. Amos, the farmer-turned-prophet, noted his people's ruthlessness toward the orphan, widow, and immigrant. In the face of such poverty he was shocked by the luxury of the palaces and mansions of the rich. "Woe to those who lie upon beds of ivory…and eat lambs from the flock…who sing idle songs to the sound of the harp…and anoint themselves with finest oils, but are not grieved over the ruin of Joseph" (Amos 6:4–6). Amos made it clear that God was the one making this challenge. Divine revelation itself was taking up the cause of justice for the world.

Rabbi Abraham Joshua Heschel, renowned for his deep spirituality as well as his devotion to social justice, wrote that the impulse to justice came from God. A mystic, philosopher, and social activist, he marched for civil rights as well as peace in Vietnam. Heschel visualized the pathos of God who was the first to feel the pain of the poor and made this known to Moses. "I have seen the affliction of my people in Egypt. I have heard their cry. I know their sufferings" (Exodus 3:7). This was inhaled by the prophets as sympathy (from the Greek *syn-pathos*) for the unjustly treated.

Isaiah continued preaching the Word of God's justice as is evident in the very first chapter of his prophecies. His sermon to a crowd at the Temple scorched their devotion to a liturgy that has no connection to the moral lives of the listeners. "Trample my courts no more! Bring no more worthless offerings; your incense is loathsome to me" (Isaiah 1:13). What does God prefer? "Cease doing evil; learn to do good. Make Justice your aim: redress the wronged, hear the orphan's plea, defend the widow" (1:16). God was not opposed to liturgy; he objected to worshipers who left the Temple and continued to oppress the helpless.

Jesus proclaimed that the kingdom of God is a kingdom of love, justice, and mercy. He taught us that the best way to help the poor is to begin with the sacred dignity and image of God found in every human person. He commanded us to implement this vision with a formation of conscience that strengthened the beliefs, attitudes, and practices which make avoiding greed and helping the poor possible. His sermon on the Last Judgment in Matthew 25:31–46, is about feeding the hungry, clothing the naked, and caring for the sick as acts that are done to him. They are essential goals for Christ's just society.

His Sermon on the Mount, which begins with, "Blessed are the poor in spirit, for theirs is the kingdom of heaven" (Matthew 5:3), is yet another inexhaustible fountain of wisdom for a just society. Jesus asks us to brand his words onto our consciences: "Do not worry about your life, what you will eat, or about your body what you will wear…Seek first the kingdom of God and all these things will be given you besides…Do to others whatever you would have them do to you" (Matthew 6:25, 33; 7:12). Jesus does not ask us to be irresponsible parents or public leaders. He challenges us to trust in his mighty graces and vision for salvation. "Surrender to God's will" is his profound advice.

Treat Symptoms and Causes of Injustice

Translated into our contemporary situation, the search for justice involves treating the *symptoms* as well as the *causes* of injustice. Sometimes these two issues are pitched against each other as though caring for people's immediate needs (food, clothing, and shelter) is not as important as changing the sinful structures of society (the greedy people and unfair laws that authored our present economic breakdown). Both goals are essential. We need food pantries for the hungry and shelters for the homeless. We also need ways to help everyone make a living and provide for their families.

Two extraordinary Catholic women witnessed this two-pronged approach. Mother Teresa of Calcutta poured out her life caring for the dying, AIDS victims, and the poorest of the poor. She treated the symptoms of injustice and was acknowledged with a Nobel Prize, a speech at a Harvard commencement, and as the principal presenter at a National Prayer Breakfast with the president, vice president, and other dignitaries in attendance.

Better yet, Pope John Paul II beatified her. When she received a medal from the United Nations, she was honored as the world's most admired woman. She replied by having the dignitaries recite the Prayer of Saint Francis with her: "O Master, grant that I may never seek to be loved, but to love with all my heart."

Still, some critics asked Mother Teresa if she thought she really was successful? They said, "You take care of those old people, they die and you don't change that." She said, "Well I didn't know I was supposed to be successful. I thought I was supposed to be faithful." And there's the answer.[2]

Dorothy Day of New York City also poured out her life to care for the symptoms of poverty, but her greater witness was aimed at the injustice in our society caused by racial prejudice, economic inequality, unfair laws, poor education, and too great a fondness for war. Her cause for canonization is being sought. Though her work was unpopular among many Catholics early on, since Vatican II's *Gaudiem et Spes* her cause has found broad support within the church.

Since Harvard-educated Father Bryan Hehir's tenure at the bishops' office in Washington, D.C., the U.S. bishops have been consistently active in addressing the causes of injustice in our country. Father Hehir loves to base his moral vision on the truth that the destination of the goods of the earth are meant for all the people on earth. He has held all kinds of prestigious posts and is a regular at symposiums on the search for justice. The ripple effect of his teachings and witness has touched the curriculums of seminaries and Catholic colleges and high schools and parish pulpits.

He remains visibly a Catholic priest whether as a teacher at Harvard Divinity School or being a consultant on justice issues with heads of Foundations or government officials. His normal residence is a nearby rectory where he leads liturgy as often as his travel schedule permits.

Along with countless others, Mother Teresa, Dorothy Day, Bryan Hehir, Walter Burghardt, and Raymond Kemp would see the tragedy of our time as described by famed intellectual Jeffrey Sachs: "In our Gilded Age, the poorest of the poor are nearly invisible. Seven hundred million people live in the 42 so-called Highly Indebted Poor Countries (HIPCs), where a combination of extreme poverty and financial insolvency marks them for a special kind of despair and economic isolation."[3]

That's the problem. The solution is found in obedience to the Word of God as framed by the ancient prophets like Amos and Isaiah and by the powerful leadership of Jesus who taught, and witnessed God's kingdom of love, justice, and mercy. His saving grace in his sacred passion and death and his resurrection provide us with the freedom, imagination, and inner energy to bring justice to the world. The church's social teachings are an updated version of the Just Word of the prophets and Christ, given to us by Holy Spirit guiding the popes, bishops, priests, and the People of God. Flowing from the altar of the Eucharist are the graces of Christ in his mysteries that push us to serve the poor, the underdogs, the helpless, the orphan, the widow, and the immigrant.

. . . .

DO NOT ADORN THE CHURCH AND IGNORE YOUR
SUFFERING NEIGHBOR

Do you want to honor Christ's body? Then do not scorn him in his nakedness nor honor him here in the church with silken garments while neglecting him outside where he is cold and naked...What use is it to weigh down Christ's table with golden cups when he himself is dying of hunger? First fill him when he is hungry and then use the means you have left to adorn his table.

I am not forbidding you to make such gifts. I am only demanding that along with such gifts and before them you give alms. He accepts the former but he is much more pleased with the latter....

Will you have a golden cup made but not give a cup of water?

What is the use of providing the table with cloths woven of gold thread, and not providing Christ himself with the clothes he needs?

Apply this to Christ when he comes as a pilgrim looking for shelter. You do not take him in as your guest, but you decorate floor and walls...

You provide silver chains for the lamps, but you cannot bear to look at him as he lies chained in prison.... For those who neglect their neighbor a hell awaits with an inextinguishable fire....

Therefore, do not adorn the church and ignore your afflicted neighbors for they are the most precious temple of all.[4]

. . . .

Father Bob Cornell's memoirs are entitled *Is There a Priest in the House?* a play on words from that question more often asked about doctors. The link between priests and doctors is appropriate. Father Robert Barron, the much-admired professor of theology at Mundelein Seminary in Chicago, has preached and written widely about the priest as a soul doctor. Barron is right in a number of ways. The priest at Mass implores the Holy Spirit to come and change the bread and wine into the Body and Blood of Christ. Thus the priest is God's instrument in giving the world the divine physician, the greatest healer of souls.

In this chapter I have linked the priesthood with the church's social teachings. Besides his sacramental role, the priest can be a soul doctor for waking up Catholic consciences to the worldwide need for justice for the poor and oppressed. This begins at home in each parish and like the rainbow arcs itself to the dark regions of earth to bring hope to the hopeless, confidence to the despairing, and love to the unloved.

For Reflection

1. Father, how well have you awakened people to the Just Word?
2. What causes resistance to the church's social teachings?
3. How do you treat the symptoms and causes of injustice?
4. How aware are parishioners of scriptural teachings on justice?
5. What can we do for the victims of the current economic collapse?

. . . .

"When you see a priest, you should say, 'There is he who made me a child of God, and opened Heaven to me by holy Baptism; he who purified me after I had sinned; who gives nourishment to my soul.'"[5]

—*Saint John Vianney*

CHAPTER FOUR

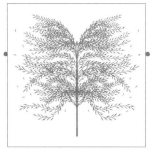

PRAYER

Dear Priest, Escape from your everyday business for a short while. Hide for a moment from your restless thoughts. Break off from your cares and troubles and be less concerned about your tasks and labors. Make a little time for God and rest in him.

Enter into your mind's inner chamber. Shut out everything but God and whatever helps you to seek him. When you have shut the door, look for him. Speak now to God and say with your whole heart. "I seek your face. Your face, Lord, I desire."[1]

—*Saint Anselm*

"MY PRIESTHOOD HAS ALWAYS BEEN A JOY TO ME. I SEE OUR PRINCIPAL JOB as priests as service to our parishioners. The laity don't look to us for great learning, but for holiness. They want us to have faith and love and respect for them."[2] These words come from the now retired Benedictine Father Arnold Weber, a priest who was pastor of Holy Name of Jesus Parish in Medina, Minnesota. He began with 250 families that grew to 2,500 families and 8,000 people.

He witnessed a liturgical spirituality but he also fostered adoration of the Blessed Sacrament, the rosary after daily Mass. He took forty young people to Medjugorje for a retreat. Did it help? He said that those that didn't pray much are now prayerful. He asked the members of the Serra Club, a group that promotes vocations, what they expected in a priest. They told him they looked for solid piety and good theology.

When the young asked him what it takes to be a priest, he replied,

> You need two things: a funny bone and a backbone. If you don't have those two, you won't make it because our culture is so different from what priests stand for. If you don't have a sense of humor, if you get depressed by the problems, you won't be able to preach the good news. You also need a backbone; if you don't, you will soon fall in line with the surrounding culture.[3]

He has a degree in marriage counseling. He spent on average twenty hours a week in that work.

Beneath his folk wisdom and remarkable achievements at Holy Name, Father Weber has been blessed with the faith that moves mountains and an integration of prayer and action that brings a blessed assurance to priests everywhere that such a dream is possible.

I find myself often saying that without prayer my priesthood and yours is an empty shell. The church calls the priest to celebrate the Eucharist and pray the Liturgy of the Hours and spend some time in meditative prayer every day. Yet I fully realize that in the light of the incredibly busy schedules of the modern American priest, due mainly to a shortage that is killing many of them, there is an exhaustion that drains the spirit from the Mass, puts pressure on praying the Divine Office with devotion and turns meditation into a struggle to resist sleep.

Most priests want to connect prayer and action and need both the motivation and the wisdom to maintain the balance. The aging of the clergy only sharpens the dilemma. Happily, a great many priests, like Father Weber, perceive the current crisis as an opportunity to rebuild and renew the church to be more rugged and flexible than ever.

With everyone else I admire the numerous examples of priests who have done wonders in their parishes, increased the membership, encouraged impressive participation by the laity, raised social awareness, adopted poor parishes, raised sums of money that would the envy of professional fundraisers, preached evangelizing homilies, promoted vocations, and sustained the devotional aspects of the faith. These priests are generally bashful when asked about their prayer life and seldom offer specific thoughts about it. Their theology of prayer is preached by their behavior. It's not unreflective, but communicated with a humility that is modest and appealing.

A Prayerful Priest: Basil Hume

My friend of forty years, Monsignor Francis Kelly, and I have twice attended the patristics conference and the Cardinal Newman Society meetings at Oxford. Through the efforts of my priest friend, we also met three times with Cardinal Basil Hume, head of the archdiocese of Westminster, which embraces London and the surrounding area. He was a gracious and welcoming host. He answered the door himself at the archbishop's house, took our coats, hung them up and made us feel at home in a large sitting room with portraits of former archbishops gazing at us.

Informally dressed in a well-worn cardigan sweater, he served afternoon tea in the English style. He spent most of the time asking us questions about the church in the United States and our opinions about hot-button issues. He never seemed eager to talk about himself. He had been president of the European conference of bishops, but he talked like a neighboring pastor.

Hard to believe, but the tenth anniversary of his death has occurred already. His nephew has edited a book of essays by friends, family, and colleagues celebrating the personal and more private side of this much-loved man. *The London Times* published some excerpts from the book under the headline, "Remembering a Man of Prayer: Basil Hume." Some of those comments follow.

In describing the various experiences he had during his daily half-hour meditation, he liked speaking to God, for example:

> I am caught between the desert and the marketplace. In the desert there is space, solitude, silence, stillness—a sense of your presence, nothing between You and me...—sometimes a Gethsemane experience, a struggle with anxieties, fears, the sense of being overwhelmed by the problems of life or just bored and distracted—sometimes a Mount Tabor experience when we can

say: "It is good, Lord, to be here." I love that desert. In the marketplace the world is present... Distractions abound and temptations too. Must I flee from the marketplace and go to the desert... and yet all those people are made to Your image and likeness—drawn to them, I am drawn to You, admiring them, I admire You, fond of them, I am fond of You...

If I don't go into the desert to meet God, then I have nothing to say when I go into the marketplace.... I could only survive my work as Archbishop...if I have allocated so much of the day to prayer.[4]

In a conference to priests he declared his inadequacy. "Deep down in every priest there is always a slight sense of unease...we discover we are in fact too fragile to carry the hopes of those we serve...I am increasingly of the opinion that no one is ever really worthy enough to exercise authority over others."

When asked if he had any regrets, he answered after a brief pause, "Time unspent. Love not given."[5]

He frequently was honest about his difficulties with prayer and composed some rules of prayer that can help us. "I have to be disciplined and ordered and stick at it. The best way to pray is the way that suits you." His rules were:

Make space every day for a quarter to a half hour for prayer.

Don't look for success.

Don't give up.

Do spiritual reading, for "the mind needs to be fed in order to stimulate prayer."

Read the Gospels as addressed to you personally.

Like the blind man, ask for sight.

Like the deaf man, ask for hearing.

Like the leper, ask to be cleansed.

Like the lame man, ask to walk.

Make distractions part of your prayer. Plan on it!

This is a priest who encountered many problems in his spiritual life especially a tendency to rely on his own efforts rather than God. "Nothing in my spiritual life do I find harder than to trust.... I don't trust God enough. I do fret. I do fall into the trap of thinking that it all depends on me."[6]

Why Spend Daily Time in the Desert?

Basil Hume gives us a good start. If we don't retire to the desert of solitude, quiet, and direct conversation with God we will not bring much to the marketplace. If we don't breathe in the Life of the Spirit, then in the pulpit, at the altar, with our breviary, in the confessional and at the sick bed we will not be able to breathe out the Spirit into these critical elements of a priest's life. Listen to Saint Paul in Romans 8. The chapter is dense, but I find that highlighting a few verses makes the point about desert and marketplace:

> Those who live according to the flesh are concerned with the things of the flesh, but those who live according to the spirit [are concerned] with the things of the spirit. Whoever does not have the Spirit of Christ does not belong to him. For those who are led by the Spirit of God are children of God.... You received the spirit of adoption, through which we cry, Abba, "Father!" The Spirit too

comes to the aid of our weakness; for we do not know how to pray as we ought, but the Spirit intercedes [for us] with inexpressible groanings. (Romans 8:5, 9, 14–15, 26)

Saint Paul uses the expression *Spirit* twenty-nine times in chapter eight. It is in contrast to our "flesh," that is, our earthbound way of living. Every priest has the same basic human struggles as every parishioner. All of us are in the same boat. We are redeemed in our baptisms. The ordained priest has the special graces of holy orders. The sacraments put us in touch with Christ and the Holy Spirit. But the "flesh," or the damage from original sin, remains to wound all of us. The *Catechism* calls it the remainder of concupiscence, an inclination to sin. This is balanced by our inner drive to God. A priest, like his flock, needs the constant purifying, amazing grace of Christ through the action of the Spirit.

I recommend that a priest should keep a Bible or at least the New Testament next to his bed and read a passage before going to sleep. Then before arising, read it again. For example, take a few weeks or more to read and reread Romans 8. If you have the time, read Father Joseph Fitzmyer's masterful commentary on Romans in the *Jerome Biblical Commentary.* You will need more than a week to sort it out, or as the popular expression goes, to break it open. Saint Paul is at his flinty best in this letter—and above all in chapter eight—not sparing us the need to pray the Word, or to be dragged into asking the Holy Spirit, "What are you saying?"

It is a humbling text for many priests, partly because a number of us do not tend to think these words apply to us. So there is a study side to dealing with the words, but more importantly, these are like the words that we are called to contemplate in our daily desert life.

We are trained to apply logic and abstract thinking to the truths of God, but that is never enough. God's Word is there to shape and transform us into Christ, to make us new men, new priests. What is ontologically true must become existentially real in us.

That is the essential role of our daily rendezvous with Christ and the Holy Spirit in the desert. We were made true priests on ordination day. But we spend the rest of our lives "becoming" priests. I heard a retreat director say to us, "Become who you are." The Holy Spirit is the divine architect drilling, carving, sanding, polishing, and etching the countenance of our basic materials into being an "alter Christus," as nineteenth-century preachers liked to say. Is this not what Paul meant when he wrote, "For those he foreknew he also predestined to be conformed to the image of his Son" (Romans 8:29)? Of course if we never stand still long enough for the artist to accomplish his goal, we will not even be an unfinished symphony. We may instead join the disappointed lost souls still waiting for fulfillment. Part of this is our male inclination to shaping others and a resistance to being formed. We like being givers, not receivers. We shouldn't worry; there is plenty of heavy lifting for us.

The Word of the Lord Came to Me

But to be more cheerful, "We know that all things work for good for those who love God, who are called according to his purpose. Those he predestined he also called. Those he called he also justified. Those he justified, he also glorified" (Romans 8:28, 30). Our daily stepping into the quiet of God's presence is like the process whereby the Old Testament prophets received God's Word. Think of all the times the prophets say, "The word of the Lord came to me." Not, "I thought up what God wants me to say," no, I received God's Word, much the same as Elijah did on the mountain when God whispered a word of eternal meaning for all of salvation history to this day.

Naturally, I do not mean God dictated the actual words, sentences, and paragraphs. Such inspirations were flashes of divinely given insights or intuitions, amazing moments when divine light illumined the darkness of given challenges. The insight from the Word leads to the words we find to spell this out for nourishing God's people.

In our few minutes a day in divine solitude, we let the Word of the Lord come to us. We allow the divine architect to complete another tiny touch-up in our lifelong conformity to Christ. Like the aristocrats of old, we are sitting for a sculpture. The holy surgeon must dig deep into our stubborn selfishness, probe the alleys of our proud resistance to God, cut out the foolishness of sin, rip away the disease in a heart that has not yet learned to love God and people with the grandeur the priesthood deserves.

But if we persistently skip our daily visits to the space of sanctification, we lose the momentum of priesthood. Prayer is a lot of things, but in the final analysis it is the daily meeting with the Father who calls us to the holy silence, the Jesus to whom we need to be conformed, the Spirit who transforms us into what our priesthood is finally all about. Just as we beg the Spirit at Mass to come and change the bread and wine into Christ's Body and Blood, so at prayer we ask the Spirit to come and conform us to the likeness of Christ. When this is happening, the fervor of our Mass, the depth of our preaching, the compassion of our absolution, the love of our parishioners, and our service to the poor and oppressed resonates with the presence of Christ. All of this is ultimately expected of our priesthood.

Saint Paul summed this up when he wrote,

> I urge you, therefore, brothers, by the mercies of God, to offer your bodies as a living sacrifice, holy and pleasing to God, your spiritual worship. Do not conform yourself to this age, but be transformed by the renewal of your mind that you may discern what is the will of God, what is good and pleasing and perfect. (Romans 12:1–2)

Father Tim Shillcox at St. Joseph Priory wrote a paper in seminary called, "The Eucharist is a Verb as Well as a Noun." The priest is meant to be a man of sacrificial love, to be the bread that is broken for others, to be the wine that is poured out and shared with others. This is living the Mass as well as celebrating it. We verbalize Eucharist by witnessing it. Paul said it best: "Offer your bodies as a living sacrifice." That ideal is born and bred through our daily encounter with God in the holy ground where the flame of the burning bush is prepared to transform that new priest we once were into the fullness of Christ over a lifetime.

· ·

THE HOUR THAT MAKES MY DAY

Just before my ordination the thought struck me, "Why not make an hour of adoration in the presence of the Blessed Sacrament every day?" I began that practice the following day and have continued it for over sixty years.

The purpose of the Holy Hour is to encourage deep personal union with Christ. The holy and glorious God is constantly inviting us to come to him, to converse with him, to ask for such things as we need, and to experience what a blessing it is to give self entirely to Christ.

Sensitive love or human love tends to decline with time, but divine love does not. The first is concerned with the body that becomes less and less responsive to stimulation, but in the order of grace, the responsiveness of the divine to tiny human acts of love intensifies.

Neither theological knowledge nor social action alone is enough to keep us in love with Christ unless both are preceded by a personal encounter with him.

I have found that it takes some time to catch fire in prayer. This has been one of the advantages of the Holy Hour. It is not so brief so as to prevent the soul from collecting itself and shaking off the distractions of the world.

Sitting before the Presence is like a body exposing itself to the sun to absorb its rays. In those moments one does not so much pour out written prayers, but listening takes its place. We do not say, "Listen Lord, for thy servant speaks," but, "Speak Lord, for thy servant listens."[7]

• •

Has Anyone Here Seen Kelly?

I have mentioned my friendship of many years with Monsignor Francis Kelly, a priest of the diocese of Worcester, Massachusetts. We first met in 1967 where he was taking a course at the Catholic

University of America. He took my courses in the history of catechetics and the human dimension of catechetics. After obtaining his degree, he was appointed diocesan director of religious education for the diocese of Worcester. By then I was director of the department of religious education at the NCEA. I needed board members for the department and I asked Frank and he accepted. He was an enthusiastic presence, cheerful, friendly, and an intelligent contributor to the cause. In 1979 when I completed my service at NCEA, Frank succeeded me as director. All this was accompanied by an enduring friendship.

I came to know what a deeply prayerful man he was and is. Over the years we have had hundreds of conversations, especially during our daily walks during the nine years I served with him at Blessed John XXIII Seminary. We seldom talked in depth about prayer. Yet I knew he devoted an hour to meditation every day and in addition was faithful to daily Mass, the Liturgy of the Hours, and the rosary. Every evening he prepared for the next day's liturgy, reading the lives of the saints, checking commentaries for the Scripture readings, keeping notes on the great solemnities.

Given his contemplative bent, he is practically an honorary member of the Trappists' Spencer Abbey where he has made dozens of retreats and weekend getaways. Despite his many professional demands, such as today being rector of the Casa Santa Maria in Rome, he makes his devoted prayer life look easy—a sign of how he has let Christ and the Spirit shape his life. I have been enriched in a thousand ways by his example of prayer, which demonstrates its possibilities.

He is not gloomy. He laughs easily and heartily, has a Churchillian appetite, and thrives on church life as well as enjoying the political theater in which the players change but in roles that are often similar. It is a privilege to experience God's graces work so well in a fellow priest.

For Reflection

1. How have you matured in your prayer life?
2. Who has influenced the way you pray?
4. What was your family's impact on your prayer?
5. How do you manage the tension of action and time for prayer?

• •

O priest...Your are not of yourself because you are the servant and minister of Christ.

Your are not from yourself because you are nothing.

What then are you? Nothing, and everything.[8]

—*Saint Norbert, Founder of the Norbertine Order*

CHAPTER FIVE

PRIESTLY IDENTITY

I CAME TO AUSCHWITZ ON A WARM AND CLOUDLESS DAY, SEPTEMBER 20, 1997. Groomed gardens and green trees surround the entrance. Grass and bushes border the red brick buildings that had been barracks for the Polish army before the Nazis took it over. The buildings contain exhibits, pictures, and mounds of hair, eyeglasses, shoes, and suitcases saved from the victims. This is the real Holocaust museum. From the outside the tidy place is peaceful. Inside, it is a house of horrors.

I arrived at what was called the death block, a U-shaped space between the last two barracks connected by the wall of the prison. Here the firing squads passed their days shooting people to death. The building to the left was an infirmary where the sick listened to the gunfire all day long and the desperate moans of the dying.

The building to the right housed a basement prison for those destined to be shot. The cells were empty and barren, except the cell of Saint Maximilian Kolbe. Flowers and candles carpeted his cell—signs of beauty, nobility, and heaven in this manmade hell. Kolbe's saintly humanity mysteriously reaches out to the millions of innocent men, women, and children who were murdered in this camp.

Praying at his shrine I thought of that day in 1941 when a siren sounded to announce that a prisoner had escaped. The guards convened the inmates. Ten would be chosen for starvation in reprisal for the escapee. Slowly the commander strolled through row after row picking the ten. The last man, Francis Gajowniczek, wept openly and cried out, "My wife and my children!" Father Kolbe broke ranks and walked to the front of the assembly.

"I want to speak to the commander."

"What do you want?"

"I want to die in place of that prisoner."

"Who are you?"

"I am a Catholic priest."

"Request granted."

The ten men had been taken to the basement death block. They were stripped and left to starve. "You'll dry up like tulips," said the guard. Kolbe encouraged the men, "Hold on, the escapee may be found." He led them in prayer. Two weeks later four were still alive, Kolbe among them. A doctor came and injected them with carbolic acid. Death came in less than a minute. It was the eve of the Feast of the Assumption of Mary.

The young Kolbe had written to his mother, "I pray I may love without limits." God heard his prayer. What happened to the man he saved? He survived Auschwitz and attended Father Kolbe's canonization in 1982.

Archbishop Timothy Dolan cited Father Kolbe's story as a compelling example of a priest who was not confused about his identity. Noting that Kolbe's answer to the guard was not his name or nationality, Dolan wrote:

> His response was simply and humbly, "I am a Catholic priest."
>
> In the eyes of God, in his own eyes, in the eyes of God's Church and his suffering people, Maximilian Kolbe's identity was that of a priest. At the core of his being, on his heart, was engraved a nametag, which marked him forever as a priest of God. That identity could not be erased by the inhuman circumstances of a death camp, or the godless environment of Auschwitz, or by the fact that Father Kolbe was hardly "doing" the things one usually associates with priestly ministry, or that the people around him had mostly lost any faith or recognition of the supernatural they may have had before they entered that hell hole.
>
> ...That identity came from God, and was imbedded indelibly within, born of a call he had detected early on from the Master to follow him and sealed forever by the sacrament of holy orders.[1]

Fathers, Who Are We?

Father Kolbe, God bless him, had no crisis of priestly identity. He laid down his life to save another prisoner and clearly told the guard, "I am a Catholic priest."

When I was ordained in 1953 I did not question my identity. I wore the collar and the black clerical suit as a sign of priesthood. It never occurred to me that my calling was temporary. I was a priest forever, like Melchizedek. Yes, I was wet behind the ears and innocent of the challenges that awaited me. And yes, I liked the movie priests such as Bing Crosby's Father O'Malley civilizing the inner-city kids. I was inspired by Spencer Tracy's rugged Father Flanagan, whose Boys Town was symbolized by the statue of a boy carrying another one his shoulders with the words, "Father, he ain't heavy. He's my brother."

In the years that followed, we all witnessed thousands of priests losing their identity and leaving the priesthood. We heard of the temporary priest and the priest whose identity is no different from anyone else in the church. The sex abuse scandal added to the confusion and self-doubt of many priests and potential priests. Seminaries thinned out. The priest shortage intensified.

In the relentless assault on priestly identity from 1965 to the present, I was encouraged by the words of Habakkuk 3:17–19, recited or sung in Week II at Friday Morning Prayer:

> For though the fig tree blossom not, nor fruit be on the vines,
> Though the yield of the olive fail, and the terraces produce no nourishment,
> Though the flocks disappear from the fold, and there be no herd in the stalls,
> Yet will I rejoice in the Lord and exult in my saving God.
> God, my Lord is my strength,…and enables me to go upon the Heights.

This was Habakkuk's song, though all the fruitfulness of his farm and flocks had vanished. Instead of tears and self-pity, he rejoiced in

God. He finished his prophecy on this upbeat note, affirming his confidence in God. Habakkuk persevered amid discouraging conditions that threatened the livelihood of his family.

Pointing to the jubilee year for priests, Pope Benedict held up Saint Paul as a splendid model. "Saint Paul is an example of a priest who was conscious of possessing a priceless treasure, that is, the message of salvation, but in an earthen vessel. He is at the same time strong and humble, intimately persuaded that everything is God's doing, everything is grace."[2]

If our culture makes it hard to be a priest, criticizing our calling, telling us we should be married, confronting us with the scandal of fellow priests, disrespecting our teachings, disparaging us for defending life, marriage, and family and condemning us for our views on stem-cell research, gay lifestyle, and immigration as being somehow un-American, we might remember Saint Paul's list of complaints in 2 Corinthians 11:16–31:

Five times receiving forty lashes minus one. Stoned once.
Numerous brushes with death.
Three times shipwrecked.
Frequently in jail.
Sleepless nights. Starving. Thirsty. Freezing.
Threatened with dangers by robbers, rivers, gentiles, his own people, the desert, the sea, traitorous brothers.
On top of it all, a thorn in the flesh.

We have some hard times, but Paul's troubles were far greater and his interpretation of difficulties is what we need to cope with our challenges. None of his hardships lowered his commitment to the priesthood. Even when he finally broke down and asked God at least to remove the thorn in the flesh, he survived God's refusal and was able to say with faith:

> I will rather boast most gladly of my weaknesses, in order that the power of Christ may dwell with me. Therefore, I am content with weaknesses, insults, hardships, persecutions and constraints, for the sake of Christ; for when I am weak, then I am strong.
> (2 Corinthians 12:9–10)

The last forty-plus years have witnessed a shrinking priesthood, but it has also been the period of the teachings of Vatican II on the priesthood, the twenty-five years of that indomitable priest Pope John Paul II, his Apostolic Exhortation *Pastores Dabo Vobis*, the signs of new vocations in the seminaries and dioceses, the wisdom of Benedict XVI, and World Youth Days, from which 25 percent of present-day vocations have come.

What is our identity? A priest is more than an enabler and facilitator. Priestly identity is rooted in our faith and the mystery of Christ. Priests serve Christ, act in his name, and strive to lead people to be disciples of Christ. As priests we are ambassadors for Christ. At our ordination the Holy Spirit, through the ministry of the bishop, conforms us to Jesus Christ as head of the church. Holy orders is a sacrament sanctifying our commitment to build up the church.

From this sacrament we receive the character of holy orders. The character signifies God's permanent covenant with the church and with us in this sacrament. Since God will never abandon us, we are expected to be faithful priests always. In living the character we reject the idea of a temporary priesthood and promise that we will remain faithful to our priesthood, with God's help, until death.

Saint Paul's fidelity to Christ is his way of reflecting on the sacramental character of priesthood, though he was not formally using the concept. An excellent example is found in his very personal note to Timothy. Facing death and determined to remain faithful to Christ, he uses the image of the eucharistic chalice, writing, "For I am already being poured out like a libation and the time of my departure is at hand. I have competed well. I have finished the race. I have kept the faith" (2 Timothy 4:6–7). This is the meaning of the ordination character. God was always faithful to Paul. Now it is clear that Paul's fidelity has lasted his life time. He kept the faith. "From now on the crown of righteousness awaits me" (4:8).

• •

REDISCOVERING PRIESTLY IDENTITY

Father Robert Lacombe of Rhode Island says, "I felt very strongly that a call to the priesthood was something whereby I could serve Christ and help to redeem the image of the priesthood and give the Church added credibility."… He felt Catholicism "would need articulate, clear, and intelligent spokesmen to defend the teachings of Christ and to represent his Church in the world…I don't look upon myself as a savior of the Church. The Lord will do that through the Holy Spirit. Nevertheless, to a degree I can cooperate in that."

Lacombe wears a collar not only as a statement but an invitation. He recounted an incident that occurred when he was visiting the historic Cathedral of St. Louis in New Orleans. While Lacombe was walking along the Stations of the Cross, a stranger approached him, said he was Baptist, but asked if they might talk. They sat in a back pew, where the priest learned the man was greatly distraught over his sister, whose dissolute life had recently ended in suicide. "I spent about an hour talking with this man and answering his questions, some of which had no answers," he says. As they parted, Lacombe handed the man his card. Back in Rhode Island a few weeks later, the priest received a letter from him, saying their conversation had finally given him some peace about the tragedy. "Now, if I wasn't dressed as a priest," said Lacombe, "he would have had no reason to come up to me."[3]

* *

Father Blaise Peters—A Focused Priest

A younger member of my community, Father Peter Renard, served as an assistant in St. Joseph's Parish with Father Blaise Peters. Any time Blaise's name comes up, Father Renard invariably says, "A helluva priest!" For him Blaise was an exemplary pastor, always busy—an "Energizer bunny"—and pastoral. Renard says, "What I admired most about him was that when I came to him with a message or a question, he would drop everything and give me his undivided attention. He was focused."

I agree with Father Renard. For my first four years after ordination in 1953 I was assigned to St. Joseph's parish in De Pere, Wisconsin. Father Blaise Peters was the pastor. The parish church served both the local parishioners and also the needs of St. Norbert Abbey and St. Norbert College. While I was full-time at the parish I also taught in our high school. There was also a parish school cared for by the Sisters of Saint Joseph.

Father Blaise lived up to the fiery image set by his name, ardent in serving the people and quick to deal with the complexities of the needs of the abbey and the college. He was a slightly late vocation, having been trained as an accountant before entering our seminary. He had a sturdy build and a commanding voice.

We were appointed to the parish at the same time. One of Father Blaise's first goals was to visit almost every home and apartment in the parish boundaries. He introduced himself personally to all the parishioners and some potential members.

We lived in a small rectory across the street from the church, and we ate our meals in the abbey next to the church. Each evening after supper Blaise invited me to sit for half an hour and talk about our day. TV had yet to become a normal distraction. He explained what he was doing and I did the same. Between my questions and his comments I was receiving a firsthand pastoral seminar from a pro.

The rest of the evening he was giving marriage instructions, counseling married couples, instructing those interested in the faith (this was before the RCIA program), helping those returning to the church, or updating the budget. There were three hospitals in Green Bay where Blaise visited parishioners, often three times a week. He was passionate about hearing confessions, not just on the regular Saturday afternoons and evenings, but also before each of the two morning Masses on weekdays.

He used First Thursdays as a chance to visit the sick and elderly in their homes to hear their confessions and chat with them a bit. It was my duty to bring them Communion on the First Fridays. I liked it, but did not have time to visit since I had to get to my classes at the high school.

Of course all work and no play makes anyone dull. I was able to take time away, but Blaise seldom did except to see his family who lived in the area. I finally persuaded him to take a week's vacation by agreeing to accompany him. This became an annual visit to northern Michigan, where we met with Norbertine pastors.

After four years I was assigned to help with novice formation. Blaise soldiered on, eventually relocating the parish to a forty-acre plot where he built a school, convent, and small chapel. Sunday Masses were in the gym. He retired from the parish at seventy and took a post as a chaplain at St. Joseph Hospital, Eureka, California. For the next fifteen years, he visited every patient every day, informing clergy from other faiths when one of their flock fell ill. At eighty-five he finally let go and let God take him from this life, at ease with his identity to the last.

He was always a parish priest at heart and he made many close friends with the diocesan clergy. When Abbot Killeen suggested that Blaise teach at the college, he replied, "I would rather take a slow boat to China." He admired the college, but preferred parish service. To use a pun, he was a "Trail Blaiser," often creative and assured. I asked him how he would increase income in the parish. His standard answer was, "Give the people plenty of service and they will respond. I will only give one money sermon a year." That's what he did and it worked. The long line of people at his wake and funeral showed that he was not forgotten and constantly blessed. I heard them say: "He saved our marriage… He showed us how to manage our finances… He never forgot me when I was sick… He made my becoming a Catholic a joy… He helped me to forgive."

Because of Father Blaise Peters I always had a love of parish life and admiration for the diocesan priesthood, even though I never again served in that capacity. Yet for most of my life I have helped out in parishes especially on weekends. And for nine years prior to my golden jubilee of priesthood, I taught at Blessed John XXIII Seminary where we train older men for the parish priesthood.

Our brotherhood has been pruned a lot, but then pruning usually yields fresh branches and new life and I believe that it is happening now.

Reflect

1. What challenges about priestly identity do you see today?
2. Which priests do you admire for their confidence in their calling?
3. How have you overcome any problems with priestly identity?
4. What do you do to attract vocations to the priesthood?
5. How do you respond to challenges to the priesthood?

• •

Christ, our high priest,

with Saint John Vianney, patron of priests, we pray that our priests will never fail to lead us to you.[4]

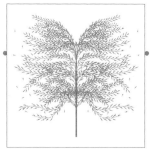

CHAPTER SIX

FAITH-FILLED AND FAITHFUL PREACHING

Let me share with you the opening parts of a homily given at the golden jubilee of a priest. I was present for the celebration and asked the homilist for a copy and obtained his permission to quote from it.

> When you become a priest you never know what your life will be like. I guess we're not really unique in that regard. You think you know, but you really don't. And that's probably a good thing, because if you knew you might think you won't have the strength or the faith to do it.
>
> You know you'll say Mass and hear confessions. You know you'll officiate at weddings and funerals and baptisms and the other sacraments, and you look forward to those times. You don't realize you might have to comfort the parents of a small child

who drowned in the family pool, or those of a teenager who thought he could drive like Dale Junior but died only a couple of days after his sixteenth birthday.

You don't realize you will be the chief maintenance man, book-keeper, office manager, and liturgist in a parish that could have a few hundred families or several thousands.

You could never imagine the unusual things that will happen along the way and some of the requests you will receive—like the man who came to confession carrying his two pet monkeys, the bride who carried her dog down the aisle on her wedding day, the bride who wanted to fill the church with miniature orange trees, or the child who suggested to Mary and Joseph during a Christmas liturgy that they should try another hotel—the inn was fully booked and they probably could not afford to stay there, anyway! All these happened here at St. Edward [during Father Frank's tenure].[1]

The Purpose and Practice of Preaching

The Risen Jesus commissioned the apostles to preach and teach all that he had commanded them. "Go, therefore, and make disciples of all nations, baptizing them in the name of the Father and of the Son and of the Holy Spirit" (see Matthew 28:18–20).

In this passage Jesus emphasizes teaching people his gospel in all its meanings so they will come to faith in him, receive baptism and become his disciples. This teaching has truths and the application of these truths to Christian behavior. For Jesus this teaching stirs up a personal relationship between him and the listener. His last words in Matthew highlight the truth that Jesus is not disappearing from the earth, but abiding with them in a new and mysterious way: "I am with you always."

The Gospels portray Jesus teaching and preaching constantly. Many today like to remember the advice of Saint Francis of Assisi that we should preach always, and sometimes use words. The call to preaching by word and deed is not an either-or command; it's a both-and requirement of a priest. We are obliged to preach homilies at Sunday liturgies and urged to give brief homilies for daily Mass. Every homily contains seeds which plant a lifelong conversion in the minds and hearts of our people.

Peter's First Sermon

Look at the first Christian homily given by Peter on the day of Pentecost. After nine days of prayer with Mary, the apostles, and disciples, Peter has just been filled with the Holy Spirit in the Upper Room. The joy of the Spirit in his heart rushes to his lips. He sees before him a large group of Jewish pilgrims who have come to celebrate the Jewish feast of Pentecost. They come from all over Galilee and Judea as well as from Jewish colonies in Asia Minor, North Africa, Greece, and Rome.

Peter quotes from the Hebrew Scriptures lines familiar to his listeners. He cites the prophecy of Joel who predicted that in the final age of history God would pour out his Spirit on all people. Because of receiving the Spirit, "Your young men shall see visions, your old men shall dream dreams...Everyone shall be saved who calls on the name of the Lord" (Acts 2:17, 21).

Joel said that signs and wonders would accompany this appearance of the Spirit. Peter wastes no time, getting right to Christ. It was Jesus who performed signs and wonders which many of them saw.

"God has made him both Lord and Messiah, this Jesus whom you crucified" (2:36). Peter confronted their consciences. When they heard Peter they were cut to the heart. "What are we to do?" Peter said to them, "Repent and be baptized in the name of Jesus Christ for the forgiveness of your sins; and you will receive the gift of the Holy Spirit" (2:37–38). Acts reports that about three thousand persons were added to the church that day.

Peter's sermon contains all the essential elements of a homily. Peter's sermon led the listeners to repentance, faith, salvation, and the reception of the sacrament of baptism and life in the Holy Spirit. Most of our listeners are already baptized. Our homilies are meant to lead our people to receive the Eucharist with faith, repentant hearts, and a resolve to live as bread broken for others and wine poured out in love, justice, and mercy. With the Bread of Life we also receive life in the Holy Spirit and the abundance of the Spirit's gifts (1 Corinthians 12:14). Through Peter's sermon the Holy Spirit formed a Christian community. "They devoted themselves to the teaching of the apostles and to the communal life, to the breaking of the bread and to prayers" (2:42).

Cardinal Levada: The Homilist Is a Teacher of the Faith

On February 12, 2008, Cardinal William Levada addressed a meeting of forty bishops with a keynote address entitled "The Homilist: Teacher of the Faith." He cited Pope Benedict XVI's Apostolic Exhortation *Sacramentum Caritatis*, 46, on homilies. Here is a summary:

The quality of homilies needs to be improved.... Ordained ministers must prepare the homily carefully, based on an adequate knowledge of sacred Scripture.

Generic and abstract homilies should be avoided. Ministers should preach in such a way that the homily relates the word of God to the liturgy and the life of the community. The catechetical aim and moral application of the homily should not be forgotten.

During the liturgical year, homilists should teach the great themes of the Christian faith as proposed by the magisterium in the four "pillars" of the *Catechism of the Catholic Church,* namely, the profession of faith, the celebration of the Christian mystery, life in Christ, and Christian prayer.

The cardinal then discussed whether the homily is place for instruction, saying there should be no opposition between a scriptural/liturgical homily and a doctrinal homily. Before Vatican II it was common for dioceses to publish sermon outlines with topics that had no reference to the Scripture readings and prayers of the Masses. The Constitution on the Liturgy addressed this concern by stating that in homilies "the mysteries of faith and the guiding principles of the Christian life are expounded from the sacred text throughout the liturgical year" (52).

But the pendulum swung too far the other way, with a tendency to exclude doctrine and catechesis from homilies. Cardinal Daneels, archbishop of Brussels, says, "Liturgy is neither the time nor the place for catechesis." In responding to this, we do not advocate a return to sermons unrelated to the Sunday readings. We need to recover the teachings of the faith and integrate them into the scriptural and liturgical aspects of the homily. The homily is not simply catechesis.

The homily is part of the ministry of the Word. In preaching Scripture we need to know the exegesis, which is the meaning of Scripture, and the hermeneutics, which is the application of Scripture to the life of our people. The cardinal cited a homily he heard on Christ's encounter with the woman taken in adultery. The priest gave a good exegesis, but missed the hermeneutics. He might have applied it to the sacrament of confession. Jesus gave her mercy and advised her "to go and sin no more." Failure to preach on confession in this story or that of the Prodigal Son may account for the decline of the sacrament of reconciliation today.[2]

The Gospels Are Historically Trustworthy

Cardinal Levada commented on the prevalence in some areas of an exegesis that is overly skeptical. Quoting Father Robert Barron, he agreed that preachers sometimes undermine confidence in the truth of Scripture with comments such as, "We can't say for sure what happened here, but we know that something happened." *Dei Verbum* opposes such skepticism,

> Holy Mother Church has firmly and with absolute constancy maintained and continues to maintain that the four Gospels whose historicity it unhesitatingly affirms, faithfully hand on what Jesus the Son of God, while he lived among men and women, really did and taught for their eternal salvation…The sacred authors, in writing the four Gospels…retained the preaching style, but always in such a fashion that they have told us the authentic truth about Jesus. (*Dei Verbum*, 19)

In making an important point that doctrine is not something added to Scripture, the cardinal cited Avery Dulles:

> Doctrinal definitions are normally based on a convergent use of many biblical texts, prayerfully read in the tradition of worshiping Church under the light of the Holy Spirit.... The theological meaning of the text is a true meaning of the text and cannot be dismissed as eisegesis, as if the Church were reading into the text that which is not really there.[3]

The People Need Faith

The homilist is often urged, and rightly so, to apply his message to the needs of the people. For example, an economic crisis that causes job losses and home foreclosures will affect family life, marriages, and children's health and education. A priest must be sensitive to the material needs of his people. But there is a general spiritual need for all our people, especially in the face of the powerful influence of a secular culture. Our people need to grow in faith, not just today, but always. At baptism we are asked, "What do you ask of God's church?" The answer is, "Faith." "What does faith offer you?" "Eternal life."

Doctrine always calls us to personal and ecclesial faith. In some parishes, the truths of the Nicene Creed are chanted and the people respond to each truth by singing, "We do believe. This is our faith. This is the faith of the church. We are proud to profess it in Christ Jesus, our Lord." The whole assembly is invited to sing or say this after the profession of faith at baptisms and confirmations.

Our people need to profess their faith openly and with each other, especially at Eucharist. Our people need to hear the homilist articulate the faith early and often. The cardinal was forceful on this

issue: "It is my contention that the homilist is an indispensable figure in ensuring that Catholics do not become strangers to the faith
of the Church. To help his people know and live the riches of the
faith of the Church, which is 'their faith,' the homilist needs to think
and preach doctrinally."[4]

· ·

A PORTRAIT: FATHER FRANK

Everyone knows him as Father Frank. Originally ordained for the
diocese of Erie, Pennsylvania, he later was a priest for Miami,
Florida, and finally for Palm Beach. In addition to lifelong involvement in parish life, he also taught at the Boynton Beach Seminary
and the University of Miami and has perennially held posts in the
diocesan offices. He has been pastor of St. Edward's since 1992.

He loves being with people and maintains a special relationship with fellow priests with whom he meets constantly. He
attends to the needs of the poor and joins his parishioners weekly
making sandwiches for a nearby food pantry. He has been an
angel for the local convent of the Little Sisters of the Poor. He has
taught me the value of generosity and what a treasure that is in
the life of a priest. He likes to give and not to take.

He has a great sense of humor and loves to cook. Monday
through Friday, he cooks lunch for his staff and guests. Sunday he
cooks dinner for his priest friends and guests. His homilies fit the
ideals outlined by Cardinal Levada, working from the readings
and themes of the liturgy and weaving in faith and practical appli-
cations gleaned from his pastoral experience.

In his vision it all boils down to love, which is not, for him, merely emotion, but a lived and challenging experience. He lives in one of the richest towns on earth, but he never forgets the hungry, homeless, and poor of neighboring West Palm, nor does he forget his modest roots in Bradford, Pennsylvania.

· ·

For Reflection

1. What happens to our people when they are not called to faith?
2. Why is the "faith of our people" one of their greatest needs?
3. What do most priests think a homily should be?
4. How do you link liturgy, doctrine, Scripture, and application?
5. What do your parishioners expect from your homilies?

· ·

"The word is near you, in your mouth and in your heart (that is, the word of faith that we preach), for, if you confess with your mouth that Jesus is Lord and believe in your heart that God raised him from the dead, you will be saved." (Romans 10:8–9)

CHAPTER SEVEN

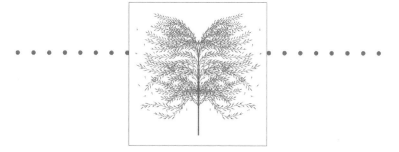

FORGIVENESS

IT WAS A MELLOW ITALIAN AFTERNOON IN ST. PETER'S SQUARE. A CHEERFUL crowd awaited its turn to see Pope John Paul II ride through their area. His Jeep was heading toward the bronze gate when the pope signaled it to pause. He leaned out to pick up a little blonde girl whose parents lifted her up to him. Two-year-old Sara held the string of a red balloon. The Holy Father raised her up for everyone to see, kissed her, and gave her back to her mother and father.

It was May 13, 1981. The time was 5:19. The assassin fired the first shot. The bullet entered the pope's stomach, pierced his colon and tore other tissue until it left his body and landed in the Jeep. A second bullet touched his elbow and broke his left index finger. The pope's secretary, Father Stanislaw, who was in the Jeep with him, caught him as he fell. He saw a young man with dark features trying to escape from the crowd. It was Ali Agca, the would-be assassin.

The driver took the Holy Father to the Vatican health services to await an ambulance to take him to Gemelli hospital. Once he was aboard the ambulance the ride was hampered by rush-hour traffic and the failure of the siren. At the hospital the doctors gave him several blood transfusions. Father Stan anointed him. The doctors believed he would not survive, but after a five-and-a-half-hour surgery, the prognosis looked better.

Recovery took several months. As he grew better he began thinking about the coincidence of the two events of May 13, the first being the original vision of Mary at Fatima, the second when someone tried to kill him. He asked to see again the Third Secret that Mary communicated to the children. After reading it, he concluded that the secret referred to his own destiny, for his life had been given back to him through the intervention of Mary. He said, "One hand shot and another guided the bullet." On his next pilgrimage to Fatima, he brought the bullet which now rests, forever harmless, in Mary's crown.[1]

John Paul as a Forgiving Priest

Almost three years later, during the Christmas season, *Time* magazine featured an unusual picture. Two men sat on metal chairs in a jail cell. One was a young man wearing a black turtleneck sweater, blue jeans, and white running shoes. The other was much older, wearing a white robe and skullcap. Pope John Paul II had come to visit Ali Agca. They were virtually knee to knee, the Holy Father holding the hand that held the gun that pumped two bullets into his body.

From our perspective it looked like face-to-face confession, but it was not that. They met for twenty minutes. Occasionally there was laughter. At the end, Ali Agca pressed the pope's hand to his forehead in a gesture of respect. The pope forgave him for the shooting. What did they talk about? The Holy Father said, "That will have to be a secret between him and me. I spoke to him as a brother whom I have pardoned and who has my complete trust."

Did the pope influence Ali? One year later Ali announced that he renounced terrorism to become a man of peace. He traced his conversion to his visit with the pope. He said he has become a devout Muslim with deep respect for Christianity. He promised that if he were freed he would preach peace in the world.

Forgiving Priests Hear Confessions

What was the first major thing Jesus did on Calvary? What was his first major act after he rose from the dead? In the devotion of the Seven Last Words of Christ, we see him on the cross, his body beaten, his head numb from the thorns, his hands stinging from the nails. What does he hear? The crowd jeers, the priests yell, the soldiers grunt—altogether now, "If you are a messiah, a king, a savior, come down from the cross!" Jesus had preached, "Love your enemies and pray for those who persecute you" (Matthew 5:44). When Peter asked him how often he should forgive someone who sins against him, seven times seven? Jesus replied, "I say to you not seven times, but seventy times seven" (Matthew 18:22, *RSV*). On the cross Christ's first words are, "Father, forgive them for they know not what they do" (Luke 23:34).

Jesus began his crucifixion with the very purpose of his imminent death, forgiving people's sins and giving them the Holy Spirit of

77

divine life. Now fresh from the grave, risen from the dead at dawn on Easter Sunday, that very night he appears to the eleven apostles and calms them with a word of reconciliation, "Shalom. Peace be with you." He reminds them that the Father had sent him to save people from sin. Now he sends them for the same mission. How? He breathes on them. That breath was the Holy Spirit whom he was pouring into their souls. He explains the breath, "Receive the Holy Spirit" What for? Why do they need the Spirit? How are they to carry on his mission? "Whose sins you forgive are forgiven them and whose sins you retain are retained" (see John 20:19–23).

Think of the thousands of times your words in the confessional flow from that holy night, "God the father of mercies has reconciled the world to himself, and sent the Holy Spirit among us for the forgiveness of sins." Just as he commissioned those first timid, trembling apostles to be confessors, so through the graces of ordination given to us by the church and the bishop, Christ and the Holy Spirit work through our timid and trembling selves to forgive sins and reconcile people to God.

Physician, Heal Thyself

In the second chapter of this book, I stressed that priests must identify with the passion and death of Christ as part of their celebration of the Holy Eucharist. We are the closest to the Mass. Would it not be strange that we priests be the least interested in carrying the cross? Would it not be cognitive dissonance to say, "This is my body to be given up" yet never apply that to our own lives? Our vocation includes living the Mass we celebrate. Our vocation involves becoming bread that is broken for others and wine that is poured out for others.

One of the reasons I chose Pope John Paul's forgiveness story is to explore the message, "Physician, heal thyself." Is not every confession a challenge to us to forgive others personally in our everyday life, to forgive till it hurts? Will our words of absolution be a weekly call to be ministers of mercy in every aspect of our priesthood? If we walked around our church and drove through our parish neighborhoods with hearts full of mercy, would we then be more inventive in finding ways to help more people come to confession?

When our souls are radiant with the peace of forgiving others, isn't that a source of creativity in promoting the sacrament of reconciliation? When Pope Benedict chose the feast day of Saint John Vianney, the most widely known confessor in church history, a monumental hearer of confessions, thousands every week, to announce the year of the priest did this make you think that the year of the priest is also the year of the sacrament of reconciliation? I have wondered about the role of the devotion to Divine Mercy, not just for the Sunday after Easter but for all our waking hours and its implications for the sacrament of reconciliation. People would not be thronging to Divine Mercy services if they were not in critical need of mercy.

Every priest knows there is no shortage of sin in every parish. The seven deadly sins flourish everywhere. What priest does not encounter anger, greed, pride, lust, jealousy, gluttony/addiction, dryness/acedia creeping into every household, apartment, and even the rectory? C.S. Lewis wakes us up with the news that the devil's biggest victories are with those whom he convinces there is no sin, hence no need for mercy, and to get on with life.

Whatever became of confession? Well, whatever became of sin? The poison of sin and evil is even in the nicest parts of town. We all agree we should have better health care. But who is worried about better soul care? Father Robert Barron likes to call priests "soul doctors" and that has an attractive resonance to it. Every human being at one time or another wrestles with the inner illness which is the inclination to evil, a leaning to sin. We are well aware of the intractable divisions in families, ghosts of obsessions that haunt lots of couples, the hunger for forgiveness that seems to find no solution even though it's available in your nearest confessional.

• •

THE AMISH SONG OF FORGIVENESS

On October 6, 2006, a milkman drove up to a one-room Amish schoolhouse on a farm in Nickel Mines, Pennsylvania. He lined up ten girls, shot all of them, killing five and wounding five, and then turned the gun on himself. The parents of the dead girls carried them home, removed their bloody clothes, and washed their bodies. Each family cleared out a room except for a large table on which to lay the child, and a few chairs where they sat and prayed through their anger and loss. Soon after this they went to the nearby home of the widow of the man who killed their daughters. They told her that they had come to forgive her husband and console her in this difficult hour. They asked what they could do for her and her three children and departed after giving her an affectionate embrace.

Ten days later, the Amish men demolished the schoolhouse. A month later the men, including the fathers of the deceased girls, began building a new schoolhouse out of sight from the road. The Amish openly forgave the milkman. They refused to speak badly about him. Half the people who attended his funeral were Amish. Donations from around the world poured in to help pay burial expenses for the dead and medical bills for the survivors.

Forgiveness is difficult, but it is easier when it is part of a community's life. The Amish religion emphasizes forgiveness, a process that takes a long time. Replacing bitter feelings to those who have wounded them requires the intention to do it, communal support, God's grace, and the belief that emotional forgiveness will follow in due time.

In the nearby firehouse, a painting hangs on the dining room wall. "Happier Days," by Elsie Beiler is a portrait of those Amish children playing without a care before the shooting. Five birds, remembering the five little girls, circle the blue sky above.

• •

I cite this utterly beautiful story about the Amish commitment to forgiveness especially when it hurts because it reminds us of our sacrament of forgiveness, our liturgy of mercy. Those parents buried their anger before they forgave the man that killed their daughters. I read that the whole Amish religion is built around the mercy of God and their vocation to reconciliation. How tragic it is for the Catholic church that the sacrament of reconciliation has almost disappeared since the Second Vatican Council. A full generation of Catholics have gone through their lives with little realization of the treasure of this sacrament and its merit for their lives and spiritual maturity.

One testament to a priest's commitment to this sacrament is the story of Saint Damien of Molokai. No other priest was allowed on the island where Damien ministered to those with Hansen's disease, thus, his greatest sorrow was his inability to go to confession on a regular basis. When the boat docked brining supplies, Damien would yell, "Is there a priest available for confession?" If one was there, he would shout his sins in Latin or in Dutch if the priest spoke that language.

Henri Nouwen's reflection on Rembrandt's painting of the Prodigal Son is a compelling insight into the forgiveness of God in that marvelous parable. A few years ago I attended a retreat that concluded with a talk about forgiveness and confession. At the end we listened to a song about the Prodigal Son, "When God Ran," by Benny Hester.

The song is built around a line in Luke 15:20. "He ran to his son, embraced him and kissed him." Cleverly, Benny begins with titles of God that make him so grand and unreachable that forgiveness does not seem to be in his job description: "Almighty God, the great I Am, Immoveable Rock, Awesome Lord, Mighty Conqueror." Such a God is beyond, absolutely still, but wait, "And the only time, the only time I ever saw him run was when he wanted to forgive me."

Christ Acts in the Sacraments

All priests know that when they sit in the confessional, or the reconciliation room, they act in the person of Christ (*in persona Christi*). We know it is Christ who does the forgiving. We also know that on the first Easter night Jesus chose priests, often frail and struggling with their own demons, to be his ministers of the sacrament of reconciliation. The Gospels show us the kind of men Jesus selected for this task—hardly angels, sometimes vain, occasionally ambitious, scared during the passion, huddled behind closed doors on the very night they would be initiated as confessors—to sit at the place of honor in the kingdom.

With all the news stories about priests, the shortcomings of the brotherhood are evident for all to see, much the same as in the Gospel accounts of the apostles. Yet Jesus is still arriving every day with the commission papers enlisting priests to be the channels of his saving grace in the confessional. Jesus is still breathing the power of the Holy Spirit through each priest so that Catholics may find absolution. Jesus is still saying through the lips of every confessor to a worried, hoping, confident Catholic the very words that came from his own lips on the first Easter night, "Shalom. Peace, my brother, my sister. Go in peace."

The first reconciliation room was the Upper Room where Jesus instituted the Holy Eucharist. In case we might miss the point of the Eucharist and its sacramental forecast of the passion and resurrection and, until the end of time, making present that mystery, Jesus clearly states that the wine become his blood creates the gift of salvation from sin. The pouring out of the blood of the Son of God cleanses us from sin and offers us the presiding presence of the Holy Spirit, making us participants in the life of God. It was Christ's providential will that the forgiveness of sins would be offered in the sacrament of reconciliation.

The wisdom of the church makes a sound link between the Eucharist and confession. We often say that the right disposition at Mass opens us all the more to the treasury of graces there. We do not necessarily need to confess before every Communion, but there are times when we absolutely must. Yes! Bless me, Father, for I have sinned. Then hear in the voice of the confessor, the echo of Christ's compassionate words, "I absolve you from your sins, in the name of the Father, and of the Son and of the Holy Spirit."

Go in peace!

For Reflection

1. Why should priests be forgiving men as ministers of the sacrament of reconciliation?
2. How often do you see priests reviving this sacrament?
3. When should confession precede Communion?
4. What can we learn from the Amish about forgiveness?
5. What did you learn from the pope's forgiveness of Ali Agca?

• •

O my God, I firmly resolve, with the help of your grace,
to confess my sins, to do penance, and to amend my life. Amen.[2]

CHAPTER EIGHT

DEVOTION TO MARY

PATRICK PEYTON WAS A NINETEEN-YEAR-OLD FARMER IN COUNTY MAYO, Ireland, when he decided to emigrate to the United States. He found a job in Scranton, Pennsylvania, as a janitor at St. Peter's Cathedral. A few years later he entered a seminary staffed by the Holy Cross Fathers at Notre Dame, Indiana. In his last year of theology, he faced a life-threatening case of tuberculosis.

> God made my worst and darkest hour the start of a new life full of meaning. In the middle of the night, my right lung began to hemorrhage. A doctor came and told me he thought I would die that night. I had been strong, vigorous and independent. Now, ambulance attendants placed me on a stretcher, maneuvered me down a narrow, winding stairway and raced me to the hospital. I deteriorated until the doctors said, "Try prayer. Our remedies are useless."

One of my teachers hurried to visit me. He saw me at my worst, discouraged, depressed, hopeless. "Mary is alive," he said. "She will be as good to you as you think she can be. It all depends on you and your faith." He activated my dormant faith. I asked Mary with all my heart and soul for my cure. If I survive, I will serve you and Christ for the rest of my days.

Against all odds Patrick survived, for after a series of medical tests the doctors found no trace of the disease in his lungs. Gratefully he wrote, "I am not describing a miracle. I'm giving witness to the power of Mary's intercession and the quiet, un-sensational way she works. When I heard the good news, I said, 'Mary, I hope I will never disgrace you.'"

Patrick was ordained a priest in 1941. Now he looked for a way to fulfill the promise he made to our Blessed Mother. He prayed, he thought, he wondered. Seven months later the answer came to him—the Family Rosary Crusade. He became an apostle of Mary's power in the life of the family. He became an apostle of families all around the world. He became an apostle of one of the most effective devotional prayers in the Catholic church, the rosary.

For the next fifty years, around the world, Father Patrick Peyton packed stadiums, cathedrals, parish churches, and classrooms and made films to help families find faith and confidence in devotion to Mary. In turn Mary fulfilled her role in opening hearts to Jesus Christ and his unifying and healing strength. Patrick died on June 3, 1992. His mission continues through Holy Cross Ministries, sponsored by the Holy Cross Fathers and Brothers. Buried on the community's grounds in Easton, Massachusetts, he is remembered in the Father Patrick Peyton Center as a place of pilgrimage and a way to continue his dream so often heard, "The family that prays together, stays together." When we think of the perilous state of marriage and the family today we may well turn again to Mary and the priest who understood her intercessory role in our mission to family life.[1]

A Priest's Devotion

During the Peyton years there was another priest—among thousands less known—who witnessed the role of Mary in the life of a priest and of the church. Every evening in his radio broadcast, Cardinal Cushing of Boston led his people in saying the rosary. The popular cardinal loved to say, "I pray that the Virgin Mary will get me into heaven fifteen minutes before the devil knows I'm dead." Cushing was also fond of this story:

Once upon a time, the Lord went walking though the streets of heaven and he saw a lot of people who had no business being in heaven at all. So our Lord went to Saint Peter who guarded the gates of heaven.

And he said, "Simon Peter, I'm disappointed in you. There are people here who shouldn't have been admitted, yet you let them in."

"Lord, it's not my fault. I had nothing to do with it."

"Well, who let them in?"

"I don't want to tell you, because I'm not sure how you'll take it."

"You should tell me. I have a right to know."

"All right, if you must know, I tell these folks they can't get in. But then they go around the back door and your mother lets them in."

This light-hearted story captures the worldwide love of the Virgin Mary. It is a world where one billion Hail Marys are said every day.

It is a world where well over thirty million pilgrims pour into Lourdes, Fatima, Guadalupe, Czestochowa, and other Marian sites every year. It is a world where Pope John Paul II inserted an M for Mary into his coat of arms, despite protests from experts who opined that lettering should not appear on such images. He went one step further and had a big M on the lid of his coffin.

In seminaries prior to Vatican II there was a surge of interest in Saint Louis de Montfort's *True Devotion to Mary*. The youthful Karol Wojtyla was among those who internalized that devotion so much so that he concluded most of his talks and writings with an affectionate tribute to Mary and a plea for her intercession. He held firm to that devotion throughout his priesthood, his years as a bishop, his involvement in all sessions of Vatican II and every day of his papacy. He was a son of Mary from first to last. Even when the Council fathers cautioned against excesses in this devotion, Bishop Karol retained his fervor for Mary. He knew the Council's tempering words:

> [The Council] strongly urges theologians and preachers of the Word of God to be careful to refrain as much from all false exaggeration as from too summary an attitude in considering the special dignity of the Mother of God. Let them carefully refrain from whatever by word or deed lead the separated brethren or any others whatsoever into error about the true doctrine of the Church. Let the faithful remember moreover that true devotion consists neither in sterile or transitory affection, nor in a certain, vain credulity. (*Lumen Gentium*, 67)

Cardinal Wojtyla's devotion to Mary was sound. Along with Pope Paul VI he noted the misunderstanding of the cautionary sentences of the Council in the sudden decline in devotion to Mary that followed the Council. He supported Paul VI's effort to correct a wrong interpretation of Marian devotion by giving the Blessed Mother a new title, that of Mary, Mother of the Church, on November 21, 1964.

> The Virgin Mary is acknowledged and honored as being truly the Mother of God and the redeemer. She is clearly the Mother of the members of Christ, since she has by her charity joined in bringing about the birth of believers in the Church, who are members of its head. "Mary, Mother of the Church."... This motherhood of Mary in the order of grace continues uninterruptedly from the consent which she loyally gave at the Annunciation and which she sustained without wavering beneath the Cross, until the eternal fulfillment of the elect. (*CCC*, 963, 969)

In the history of the church, doctrine and devotion have supported each other. During the Roman persecution Christians lovingly gathered the battered bodies of the martyrs and brought them to the catacombs for burial within stone coffins carved from the walls. In many cases these became the altars for the liturgies of their faith.

In third-century Alexandria the faith of the people developed a brief prayer to pray to Mary as the *Theotokos*, the God-bearer. At the Council of Ephesus in 431 this ancient faith of the church about Mary was reconfirmed. It is reported that in the evening after the bishops proclaimed this truth about Mary, there was a devotional candlelight procession through the streets of Ephesus in her honor. Mary does not demand attention to herself, but rather to her Son. The devotion to her as Mother of God is meant to stimulate faith in Jesus as the Son of God.

The magnificent gothic cathedrals of medieval Europe were invariably dedicated to Mary whose stone image displayed her sitting like a queen mother holding Jesus forward to encourage faith in her Son. She is not shown hugging Jesus to herself, but rather presenting him to us. In all scenes in the Gospels in which Mary appears, the attention is on Jesus. Her last words indicate her role, "Do whatever he [Jesus] tells you" (John 2:5).

Increasingly after the Reformation, visions of Mary occurred, always evangelical, calling for repentance and return to Christ and promoting the Eucharist in a shrine church. All authentic devotion to Mary opens us to authentic doctrine about Jesus and stirs up our faith in these truths so as to live by them. What we teach about Mary is based on what we believe about Christ. The devotion to Mary is not *adoration,* which belongs only to God. Catholic devotion to Mary is called *veneration,* that is, an honor given to the greatest of God's creatures and a recognition of the victory of God's graces in her life from her immaculate conception to her death and assumption into heaven.

. . . .

I FELT A MOTHER'S LOVE HAD TOUCHED ME

A retreat master was giving a retreat. Toward the end of it, a girl handed him a note. He put it in his pocket and forgot about it.

After the retreat he found it, unfolded it and read:

For the past eight months I have been in psychotherapy.

As a child I experienced overwhelming fear because of hatred and abuse. A major focus of my life right now is to overcome and transform that fear. The details are unnecessary, but much of my fear is centered on my mother…I had become so turned off to the concept of mothers that I consciously rejected the love of Mary, the mother of Jesus.

After your talk, I walked outside—feeling terribly alone. I prayed for the grace to break through the wall that was keeping me from trusting…I wanted to cry, but haven't in months.

You may have noticed a small round building near the cemetery. Curiosity is one of my strongest traits—I walked to it and opened the door.

When I looked inside, I was filled with fear. There stood a large statue of Mary. My first impulse was to run away in anger. But something drew me slowly to the kneeler at her feet. Then I fell to my knees, weeping into the folds of her robes.

When it was over, I felt cleansed and new. I felt willing to be a trusting child. Even more important, I felt that a mother's love had touched me, leaving in me a true desire to forgive my natural mother.[2]

· ·

Mary in the Life of a Priest

There is an old saying that you can tell a person by the company he keeps. In a certain sense that is true of a priest who stays near the Virgin Mary and cultivates her presence and influence. Jesus spent a lot more time with Mary than any other person in history. Her influence on Jesus was substantial in his earliest years. His impact on her is beyond telling. A priest who is near Mary benefits in these ways.

Mary is the mother of the faith of the priest. As Father Peyton recalls, Mary would be as good to him as his faith expects her to be. In a secular culture where a priest's faith is under fire, he will be stronger in his commitment to the faith because he lives each day with the greatest woman of faith in sacred history.

Mary was always full of grace from the moment of her conception. Though she faced lifelong challenges to her undivided love for Christ she never broke her loving relationship with her Son. A priest who cultivates a friendship with Mary is like a son to her. Near her he appreciates the power of a life of grace and so his struggle against sin and evil is positive and hope-filled.

When the brilliant Clare Booth Luce, devastated by the death of her daughter, went to see Father Fulton Sheen, she was prepared for a battle of wits about controversial church teachings. There was such a battle but it stopped when Sheen asked her to talk about the loss of her daughter. She began to shed a flood of tears. Sheen took her by the hand and led her to his private chapel and settled her before the shrine of Mary who had lost her Son in a tragic death. Our Lady of Grace touched her heart with faith. Her conversion began in earnest. A priest who faces the many trials of his parishioners and his personal life can see everything more clearly when comforted by his Blessed Mother.

Mary was the mother of the physical Christ born at Bethlehem. She could look at her Son and sing, "Blessed be Jesus Christ, true God, and true man." Forty days after Easter her Son ascended to heaven.

The apostles called Mary to join them in the Upper Room to prepare for the coming of the Holy Spirit. Their nine days of prayer were the first novena in the history of the church. Mary held the place of honor among the apostles who were Christ's first priests, or better yet, his primordial bishops. During their days of prayer they could gaze on Mother Mary and be reminded of her relationship with Jesus. Pope John Paul II often asked us to picture her at Pentecost and meditate on the mystery of the Mother and the church:

> Now at the first dawn of the Church, at the beginning of the long journey through faith which began at Pentecost in Jerusalem, Mary was with all those who were the seed of the New Israel. She was present among them as an exceptional witness to the mystery of Christ. And the Church was assiduous in prayer together with her, and at the same time contemplated her in the light of the Word made man. For when the Church enters into the supreme mystery of the incarnation, she thinks of the Mother of Christ with profound reverence and devotion. (*Redemptoris Mater,* 27)

Today's priests serve God in the church that was born in the presence of Mary and the apostles. The same Holy Spirit that manifested the church to the world continues to do so. We priests need to return to that day when God kissed the earth and made our one, holy, catholic, and apostolic church a living and enduring reality. Just as the Spirit hovered over Mary at the Incarnation, so also the Spirit hovered over Mary and the apostles at the inauguration of the church.

Our priesthood is an essential part of that continuity. We can't do it without the Holy Spirit, nor without Mary whose prayers helped to birth the church and to uphold our priesthood that the Eucharist be available for the existence of the church. Mary is a powerful partner of our priesthood in making the church effective and available for all who seek salvation from sins and the gifts of the Spirit of divine life.

Reflection

1. What has been your devotion to Mary during your priesthood?
2. Why is it important for priests to stay near Mary?
3. How does Mary as a woman of faith affect our priesthood?
4. Why does cultivating Mary's presence strengthen our priesthood?
5. How does Mary's presence at Pentecost continue today?

• •

"What do you want of me?" asked Lucia.

"I am the Lady of the Rosary.

Let them say the rosary every day."[3]

CHAPTER NINE

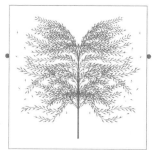

CHASTE LIVING

CATHOLIC MISSIONARIES BROUGHT THE FAITH TO JAPAN IN THE EARLY sixteenth century. Eventually the government forced them out of the country and suppressed the faith. More than two hundred years later, Jesuit missionaries came back to Japan and made an astonishing discovery of a village where about a hundred people gathered on Sundays to pray the Apostles Creed, the Our Father, Hail Mary, Glory Be to the Father, the acts of faith, hope, love, and contrition as well to recite the eight beatitudes and the Ten Commandments.

When questioned how this came to be they said the "fathers" taught their ancestors long ago to memorize these prayers and Scripture texts and gather on Sundays to say them. They also said that they expected the "fathers" to come again and teach them more about Jesus and the church. The joyful missionaries told them, "We are the 'fathers.'" The villagers were not sure about them. Needing to test them, the village leader said he had four questions for them:

"When you enter your churches, what do you do?" To their amazement, one of the fathers genuflected.

Second, does your God have a Mother?" "Yes, her name is Mary."

"Third, where does the head of your church live?" The priest replied, "Rome."

Lastly, the leader wondered, "Do you 'fathers' have wives?" All the priests declared, "No."

In the smiles, laughter and outpouring of joy the villagers took the missionaries to their hearts.[1]

Celibacy Is a Way of Loving

Priests in the Western church are called to celibacy. Not as well known by American Catholics is the fact the priests in the Eastern churches marry while their bishops must be celibate. The history of the practice of celibacy, how and why it came about, belongs to a different discussion from our current topic: chaste living.

Celibacy is often defined in a negative way as the giving up of sexual experience and a life with a wife and children. The positive view of celibacy maintains that it is a form of loving God and people with an undivided heart. Wholesome celibacy begins with the vision of the body as a temple of the Holy Spirit. A celibate should not be hostile to the body, nor treat sexuality with fear or hatred. The body and sexuality are gifts from God. If we are not accepting celibacy so we can love God and people more passionately and enthusiastically, then our celibacy will be harsh and little more than a curiosity for others.

Jesus outlined this vision of celibacy when he said, "Some are incapable of marriage because they were born so; some, because they were made so by others; some, because they have renounced marriage for the sake of the kingdom of heaven" (Matthew 19:12). Jesus himself was celibate for the sake of the kingdom which was a central theme of his message in Matthew's Gospel. Mary's virginity was related to her vocation to be Mother of God. Tradition teaches that Saint John the apostle was celibate, which many think accounts for his extraordinary emphasis on the divine presence of God in his Gospel. The mission of the undivided heart has a great deal to do with the practice of celibacy.

Lived properly, celibacy is a witness to the reality of the kingdom of God. When practiced in faith, celibacy is a way of manifesting the divine presence in the human order because of the grace accepted by the celibate. When it reflects both the love of God and the human discipline required to make it happen, celibacy beckons others to have faith in a future life in heaven and the truth of transcendent values in our secularized culture. Celibacy is at home with the supernatural life as well as everyday life.

Moreover, the celibate priest approaches sexuality as does the *Catechism of the Catholic Church:* "Sexuality affects all aspects of the human person in the unity of body and soul. It especially concerns affectivity, the capacity to love and to procreate, and in a more general way, the aptitude for forming bonds of communion with others" (2332).

The vow of celibacy, therefore, does not purge the presence of the sexual influence on "all aspects of the human person in the unity of body and soul." In this regard the celibate priest is a human person like anyone else. Above all the celibate priest adopts and develops this God given capacity to love and acquire an "aptitude for forming bonds of communion with others." Again, celibacy is for loving.

Chaste Living for Priests

The priest vows celibacy at his ordination, but the training in chaste living before that holy event is essential for taking the vow and keeping it after ordination. So it remains valuable for priests to remember the fundamentals of chaste living.

First of all, his sexuality is a matter of gender, in which the differences of maleness and femaleness abide. I recall a movement among some priests and women forty years ago called "the third way." It supported strong and affectionate relations between celibate priests and the sisters. Of course this didn't work. They played with fire and their celibacy got burned. As one comedian put it, "He knows it and she knows it, but their genes don't." Gender differences are real. Man and woman complement—complete—each other. The French phrase rejoices in the difference, "Vive la difference!"

Secondly, sexuality is also a matter of emotions, passions, feelings that accompany affectionate love and trust. The feelings are basically good but need to be part of a growth to maturity in each person. The love song that says, "It can't be bad 'cause it feels so good," is a mistaken interpretation of the real value of feelings that often give pleasure, but should only be fostered in a legitimate context.

Thirdly, sexuality is genital, a physical act that has two goals, unitive—the love of the spouses—and procreative—being open to God's gift of children. In living chastely, the celibate priest sacrifices this genital gift. His natural desire for his own children is transformed into being a shepherd, a spiritual father of many. To repeat, celibates need to acknowledge gender differences, the role of emotions, and the genital aspects of being human.

What a priest thinks of sexuality is also influenced by his family background, whether he came from loving, mature parents or has been saddled with abusive treatment whether verbal, physical, or sexual. In the latter case some priests need counseling as well as a support group. Either way, a priest benefits from a reasonable reflection on the influence of his family on his own sexuality.

The Virtue of Chastity

> Chastity means the successful integration of sexuality within the person and thus the inner unity of man in his bodily and spiritual being…The virtue of chastity comes under the cardinal virtue of temperance which seeks to permeate the passions and appetites of the senses with reason…Chastity is a moral virtue. It is also a gift from God, a grace, the fruit of spiritual effort. The Holy Spirit enables one whom the water of baptism has regenerated to imitate the purity of Christ. (*CCC*, 2337, 2341, 2345)

The celibate priest needs the virtue of chastity to stay chaste. The *Catechism* is insightful about the role of chastity as a virtuous process that integrates sexuality peacefully and successfully within a person's bodily and spiritual lives. There is little hope for chastity without the virtue. The Latin root of the word *virtue* is *vis*, meaning "force" or "power." Virtues groove the soul toward the positive ideals of priesthood. Virtues are acquired by motivational stories, good examples from the people around you, repetitive acts of chastity, and the assistance of the Holy Spirit.

The soul thrives on virtues. Where virtue is absent, obsession takes its place. Obsessive sex is unusually widespread and one of the causes is the failure to practice the virtue of chastity. The war of the flesh and the spirit, so dramatically described by Saint Paul in the seventh chapter of his letter to the Romans, is with God's help terminated by chaste living. Saint Augustine wrote that prayer is essential for chastity:

> I thought that continence arose from one's own powers, which I did not recognize in myself. I was foolish enough not to know…that no one can be continent unless you grant it. For you would surely have granted it, if my inner groaning had reached your ears and I with firm faith had cast my cares upon you.[2]

Jesus praised the power of chastity with the words, "Blessed are the pure of heart for they shall see God" (Matthew 5:8). The heart is the seat of the moral personality as Jesus said, "Out of the heart come evil thoughts, murder, adultery, fornication" (Matthew 15:19). Out of that same heart come love, justice, mercy, and purity.

No celibate priest can be pure of heart without being modest. This means honoring the privacy that comes with the sexual act and the sexual organs. Modesty affects our choice of clothes. Modesty curbs our language from being vulgar, suggestive, seductive, or crude, arousing passions or intimidating others in these areas. Modesty curtails unhealthy curiosity about sexual matters.

• •

INTERNET PORN: NOT FOR THE PURE OF HEART

Being pure of heart means that the celibate priest will avoid temptations that lead to sins against chastity. This means avoiding pornography on the Internet. Internet porn is addictive for many people and causes severe moral problems. For many men it becomes a substitute for relations with their wives and often weakens marriage to the point of divorce.

Equally so, it is extremely dangerous for the integrity of the celibate priest. Its easy access and pervasive presence is a threat to all who succumb to it. It is scandalously profitable—its revenue is larger than the combined revenues of all professional football, baseball, and basketball franchises. It can and has ruined the priesthood of many men. There are helps for a priest who finds himself caught in this trap, groups similar to twelve step programs.

Bishop Paul Loverde has published one of the best pastoral letters on the destructive nature of pornography, in which he writes, "Today perhaps more so than at any time previously, man finds his gift of sight and therefore his vision of God distorted by the evil of pornography. It obscures and destroys people's ability to see one another as unique and beautiful expressions of God's creation, instead of darkening their vision, causing them to view others as objects to be used and manipulated."[3]

* *

The Permissive Culture Opposes the Pure of Heart

Our current sex-saturated culture is hostile to chaste living. We need to counter this with promoting respect for the dignity of the human person, upholding the values of restraint, and working to change the direction the culture has taken in recent decades.

We need to find ways to counter the immoral permissiveness that is based on a false idea of human freedom. We are not free to do whatever we want. We are free to do whatever we ought. Pope

Benedict's three encyclicals drive home the idea that love and truth go together. When we deny or ignore the truth about the human person, there is little chance for authentic love and instead permission for the anything goes moral climate today.

Pope Paul VI lamented the gap between the gospel and the culture, which has resulted in the many human tragedies today especially in marriage and the family and, for the priesthood, the sex abuse scandal. The priests that fell from grace were not committed to chaste living and caused pain for those affected and damage to the credibility of the priesthood and the church. Such priests helped widen the gap between the culture and the gospel.

This needs to be turned around. There is a growing demand to replace a culture that has failed our families, marriages, and children. The bishops' creation of a charter for the Protection of Children is a positive and welcome move. It's not nearly enough yet, but some Old Testament stories remind us that God does not need big numbers to achieve his goals. Read especially the story of Gideon (Judges 7) who went out to fight the enemy with thirty thousand soldiers. God told him that was too many. Throughout a series of tests, Gideon's army was reduced to three hundred soldiers and with God's help won the battle against a huge enemy force. God's warning about too many soldiers was that, if Gideon won, he would say, "My own power brought me the victory" (Judges 7:4). It should be a salutary tale for us to recall that in 1959 we had bulging seminaries and in 1969 they were almost empty. A wise man might say, "Quality isn't everything; it's the only thing."

The Celibate Priest's Friendships

No priest is going to be productively celibate if he does not cultivate friendships. If celibacy is a form of loving God and people, and the priest has no human friends, then his celibacy will wither away and his relationship with God could be problematic. A priest without friends will either eventually lose his celibacy or become a seriously unhappy man and a curse to himself and others.

A priest's first line of friendship should be with other priests. This used to be easier when seminaries were full and classes were large enough to provide possibilities for friendship with several others. It's harder to do with fewer opportunities like that, plus so many parishes are one-priest stations that make it tough to foster friendships. Some priests are gregarious and usually solve this problem. Others are introspective and have a harder time finding a friend.

Every priest needs to be loved by others and to give love to others. Some priests naturally attract others and form friendships and community with other priests. I distinguish this wholesome approach from clerical cliques whose members often identify community in terms of exclusion. Those who are fortunate enough to be invited into a healthy circle are blessed. Many priests in these times tend to be Lone Rangers, but often become lonely rangers. Healthy and holy celibacy must be nourished by human companionship as well as personal prayer, the Eucharist, the Liturgy of the Hours, a spiritual director, a confessor, and retreats.

Another major source of friendship is our families and the laity. When we live near our families that should be a constant source of needed affection, especially if our parents are still living. Among the laity, I have been blessed with a number of couples with whom I have had a friendship for more than forty years. Their fidelity to marriage and family strengthens my fidelity to celibacy. Conversely, I believe my fidelity to celibacy has had a positive influence on their marital fidelity. I also find joy in the many acquaintances I acquire in the various places my priesthood has called me.

Celibacy is a form of loving God and others. It requires God's abundant graces, friends, modesty, purity of heart, and the virtue of chastity, which add up to chaste living.

Reflection

1. How have you found celibacy to be a way to love God and others?
2. How does the culture impede your ability to live chastely?
3. What has been your greatest support for celibacy?
4. What is the greatest joy that celibacy has given you?
5. How have family and friends supported your celibacy?

• •

And this is my prayer: that your love may increase ever more and more in knowledge and every kind of perception, to discern what is of value, so that you may be pure and blameless for the day of Christ. (Philippians 1:9–10)

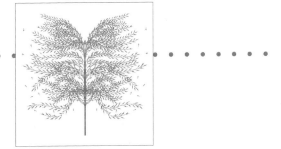

THE RESURRECTION OF THE CATHOLIC PRIESTHOOD

"A good shepherd, a pastor after God's heart, is the greatest treasure which the good Lord can grant to a parish."[1]

—Saint John Vianney

THIS MORNING I WAS READING IN A FAVORITE BLOG, WHISPERS IN THE Loggia, about good news in vocations to the priesthood. The diocese of Memphis (73,000 parishioners) will ordain six new priests this year. The neighboring diocese of Little Rock (112,000 parishioners) reports they have thirty seminarians in training—the highest count since 1966. In each case you have the "little diocese that could."

How did Memphis do it? With 25 seminarians and 73,000 parishioners, it ranks in the top five in the nation for recruits. Catholics in the city make up only 4 percent of the population. Bishop Terry Steib and Father Keith Stewart, the vocation director, keep looking and doing all they can to find young men for the priesthood. They go after recruits. They have "Evenings of Discernment" that invite parishioners to come and pray and discuss vocations. Another factor is the youth of the vocations, mostly in their late twenties, younger than the national average.[2]

It's interesting to see how God works. It's the little ones that could. God begins with the humble and shows that his grace can touch the hearts of young recruits for the priesthood. In our ordinary way of thinking we would suppose the Catholic giants would be leading the pack: New York (2.5 million Catholics); Chicago (2.1 million); and Los Angeles (4.5 million). But as Saint Paul's stinging and ringing words penetrate the myth of bigness, "When I am weak, then I am strong" (2 Corinthians 12:10), the gentle humility of the little diocese leads the way.

Jesus himself is the star of humility. Shall I say that he left the largest city in all of history (the heavenly one) and humbled himself to live with us as that brilliant song in Philippians 2:1–11 chants for us. The king of heaven disrobed himself of the status of glory to walk a simple path in a byway of the earth to lead us to glory and eternal happiness. Jesus the greatest of all priests, a high priest in the words of the Letter to the Hebrews, walked the humiliating path to the cross. Perhaps another way of saying this is: The resurrection of the priesthood begins with humility. May I quickly add, I believe the resurrection of the Catholic priesthood in the United States has begun.

It's not going to be a fad, nor should it be. We should not forget the decade after WWII when vocations jammed the seminaries. Ten years later they suddenly began to empty. We forgot that the mills of the gods grind slowly.

> Though the mills of the gods grind slowly,
> yet they grind exceedingly small.
> Though with patience he stands waiting,
> with exactness, grinds He all.[3]

Having urged this modesty of intent, I also rejoice in the signs of growth in the priesthood and fully believe a resurrection of the priesthood is welcome and long anticipated. Not just in the numbers of new members but also in the nine themes I outlined in this book, nine paths to the resurrection that is closer for us now. You could easily add many topics for discussion and I hope you do with your fellow priests. But I believe I have touched the nerve of priesthood as I myself have experienced it. Permit me to review these paths to renewal before sharing my final thoughts.

Nine Pathways to the Resurrection of the Priesthood

1. *Stay close to Jesus.* This is the first step for an enduring and fruitful priesthood. Jesus himself formed the first seminarians, the twelve apostles. He was their teacher, friend, and model. Jesus is our instructor, friend, and ideal. In the Last Supper conversation with them he used relationship words, "Love one another as I love you...You are my friends...I do not call you slaves...I have called you friends" (John 15:12, 14, 15). They are to be as close to him as

a branch to a vine. His life and theirs are bound together. Jesus asks them to have faith in him. He prays for them.

Talk about the language of intimacy and boundless challenge! That's the way he led the first priests with words of love, sacrifice, hope, and big challenges. He told them they would be hated and persecuted just like himself. In rereading this powerful conversation, I ask you to take John 14—17 and put yourself in the Upper Room and hear the words Jesus first directed to priests as if he were talking to you now.

> Not only must the scarcity of ordinations to the priesthood in certain countries not discourage us, but it must also be an incentive to increase the number of places of silence and listening to the word.... In this way God's voice, which always continues to call and to strengthen, may be heard and promptly followed by numerous young people.[4]

2. *The Eucharist.* The axiom, "No Eucharist without the priest, no priest without the Eucharist," pairs up with my first point. Jesus is the Word. Jesus is also the Sacrament. A priest who makes the Eucharist the guiding light of his priesthood will stand in a pool of light and love that gives the first answer to the question of the meaning and purpose of priesthood. Without us there is no Eucharist. Without the Eucharist the meaning and purpose of our priesthood loses its value.

> The purpose of every priest's mission is one of worship. Thus may all people offer themselves to God as a living sacrifice, holy and acceptable to him (cf. Rm 12:1)...receiving that love which they

in turn are called to offer to each other in abundance…. Love for one's neighbour, attention to justice and to the poor are not so much themes of a moral society as they are an expression of a sacramental conception of Christian morality.[5]

Fortunately we are free to be servants of Christ feeding the multitude with his Body and Blood. Church history is full of stories when the priest was banished and the people hungered for God's food. In the early days of the Reformation a priest bringing Eucharist was subject to capital punishment. In the days of the persecution of the Irish, they would gather secretly in fields around a "Mass Rock" so that the priest could bring the Bread of Angels to them. In the twentieth century, Eastern and Central Europe was the latest version of hostility to priests and Eucharist. We have the freedom to be active priests. It is a gift to our country and church and I praise God for it.

3. *The church's social teaching.* Concern for the poor is more than a matter of social morals, but is tied to the sacraments. "Through the ministry of priests, the spiritual sacrifice of all the faithful is fulfilled in union with that of Christ, the one Mediator: a sacrifice that priests offer in an unbloody and sacramental way as they wait for the Lord to come again."[6]

In reviewing the social mission of priests I think of the above quote from Benedict and the wide interest in his recent encyclical *Caritas in Veritate.* Benedict unites truth with love and also broadens social justice by connecting economic issues and life issues as part of social concern. I would hope his insights will provide the real common ground between social justice Catholics and pro-life Catholics. Priests experience the divide in parishes and among themselves. In this atmosphere of worship, *truth filled love* is not produced by us but received from God.

4. *Prayer.* This is the lifeblood of a priest. Benedictine Dom Chautard wrote that prayer is "The Soul of the Apostolate." The temptation to make "good works religion" replace taking time to pray is perennial. As Hume writes, we need to go to the desert and pray and refresh our relationship with Christ. If we don't pray we will engage in action for our own satisfaction. Instead of a way of loving God and others, we wind up loving ourselves and become disenchanted with our priesthood.

Jesus was busy preaching, working miracles, and training the apostles. Yet he went to the desert to pray and even spent whole nights on a mountain in prayer. Yes our work is a prayer also, but can easily lose that truth if we do not set aside time for prayer, especially praying the Liturgy of the Hours in a *lectio divina* manner. Prayer is still the soul of our mission.

5. *Priestly Identity.* The winds of distraction have done a lot to weaken priestly identity. How am I going to know who I am when I am constantly prodded to do what I vowed never to do? I have enough trouble with the inner moral struggles that Saint Paul marvelously describes in Romans 7. Yet the culture won't leave me be. I wake up with one person telling me I should get married. I go to sleep just after someone on TV advises me to support embryonic stem cell research. I am regularly reminded to be ashamed of the clergy sex abuse scandal. A recent movie encourages me to doubt my faith— through the mouth of a fictional priest who preaches it no less. I am

told it's time to be enlightened and get behind euthanasia. I am cursed for opposing same sex marriage. I am belittled for thinking priesthood is a lifelong commitment. Well, you know the story.

Jesus did not think priesthood was a part-time job. Jesus valued celibacy. Jesus opposed divorce and upheld marriage between a man and a woman. Father Maximilian Kolbe said it best when asked by the commander of Auschwitz, "Who are you." "I am a Catholic priest." As Yule Brunner said often in the movie, *The Ten Commandments,* "So let it be written. So let it be done."

6. *Faith-filled and faithful preaching.* I strongly recommend Cardinal Levada's ground-breaking lecture, "The Preacher is a Teacher of the Faith," discussed in chapter six. After so much confusion since Vatican II, common sense is making a comeback. Preachers need to link Scripture, liturgy, and doctrine. The cardinal is fully aware we ought to address the needs of the people, but many forget that the greatest need of people is faith. And the normal source of help for faith is the doctrine of the church which flows from Scripture and worship. *Lex credendi lex orandi.*

There are those who say the homily is no place for catechesis. Tell that to Augustine, Chrysostom, Jerome, Leo, and Gregory—the latter two popes who were called great because of their talent for catechetical preaching. We should not go back to the custom of three-year sermon outlines that had a lot of doctrine and little Scripture or liturgy.

7. *Forgiveness.* We need to forgive, to reflect the mercy of God in our personal lives, to be outstanding witnesses of forgiveness. The

attempted assassination of Pope John Paul II and his subsequent forgiveness of Ali Agca is an example of the value of being personally
merciful as well as being an absolver in the confessional. I am not
saying that the personal virtue of the priest is essential for his ministry of reconciliation. I hint that when priests explore the role of
mercy in their lives this may bring about the revival of the sacrament
of reconciliation. Surely, the example of the Amish could put us to
shame. They buried their anger before they went to the widow and
offered forgiveness for what her husband did to their daughters.
They are committed to forgiveness as the hallmark of their faith. We
can learn from them.

8. *Devotion to Mary.* In my seminary days and the first ten years of
priesthood, devotion to Mary was taken for granted and highly
esteemed. I was surrounded by it in my parish of Saint Patrick,
Rittenhouse Square, Philadelphia. I can still see the Lourdes shrine.
I can also recall twelve hundred people attending miraculous medal
services every Sunday evening during World War II. So it was more
than mildly shocking for me to hear arguments against Marian
devotion, to be told to abandon the rosary, to be mocked for defending a relationship with our (my) Blessed Mother. I guess thousands
of priests experienced this strange reaction to "The World's First
Love," in the words of Archbishop Sheen. It was like a fever, but
thanks be to God, the sickness has abated and is mostly gone. Even
evangelical Protestants are warming up to Marian devotion.

I will not be surprised to see a new priest like Father Patrick
Peyton emerge to advocate a relation to Mary for blessings on priests,
families, and children. This morning in the Liturgy of the Hours I

found just the right words to cap this reflection: "We are grateful to you, Father of mercy, for you gave us Mary to be our Mother and our model. Through her intercession, cleanse our hearts."[7]

9. *Chaste living.* My chapter on chaste living for priests belongs perfectly just after the meditation on the Virgin Mary. Throughout most of church history, celibate priests and consecrated virgins have celebrated their affinity with Mary. I find it curious that our sex-saturated culture is so upset with celibacy. In a country with nearly 300 million people, what would worry them about 65,000 priest-celibates? How does such a minuscule percentage trouble millions upon millions of Americans? Every play, movie, and novel about priests that appears is bound to have the priest break his vow of celibacy. I suppose I should be cool and agree that at least it makes for juicy storytelling even if not a piece of anti-celibacy propaganda. But there are also the news stories that are more shameless about such propaganda. The media warns us that the sex abuse scandal is a good reason for abandoning celibacy, but the U.S. Department of Justice reports that a majority of sex offenders are married or divorced.

Well enough of that. The real challenge to straying from celibacy is adopting a chaste lifestyle. I argue that priests and critics alike should understand that celibacy is a form of loving, not just living without marriage and sex. If we do not embrace celibacy for the love of God and others, what exactly would be its meaning and purpose? Jesus noted that voluntary celibacy is a witness to the kingdom of God, a kingdom of love, justice, and mercy.

I link the *Catechism* teachings about chaste living to celibacy, especially the role of the virtue of chastity and its companions, modesty in clothing and language, self-discipline in touching or looking at others, and respect for the dignity of every human person. I dwell a bit on the virtue of chastity since there was a strange resistance to virtue training by so-called progressive educators in the twentieth century. Virtue comes from the Latin *vis* meaning "power" or "strength." Virtue inclines the soul to observe behaviors that enhance character and chastity. As in other areas the power of prayer is recommended.

+ + +

Despite the reams of bad news about priests in recent years, the Catholic priesthood is a hardy plant in the garden of the church. Of all the different groups that make up the church and the state, the priesthood has a unique capacity for renewal. Better than renewal, the priesthood, so close to the heart of Christ, is bent upon another of its many resurrections in church history.

The stirrings of resurrected life can be detected at every level of priestly life. The seminaries have more students and many dioceses have more ordinations. Priests appear to be more confident and less morose about their identity. We are on the move, grinding slowly liked the famed mills of the gods. And never forget, fellow priests, Christ's last meal was with priests. He called them his friends, he shared his divine life with them and shared with them the first truths of revelation of the new covenant. We mean a lot to him.

The Good Shepherd is bringing us back.

Notes

CHAPTER ONE

1. Ignatius of Antioch, *Liturgy of the Hours* (New York: Catholic Book, 1975), p. xxx.
2. George Wilkinson, letter to author.
3. Archbishop Helder Camara, as quoted in Vicky Kemper and Larry Engel, "A Prophet's Vision and Grace: The Life of Archbishop Helder Camara," *Sojourners*, December 1987, pp. 12–15.
4. Columba Marmion, Christ: *The Life of the Soul* (Colorado Springs, Colo.: Zaccheus, 2005), p. 101.
5. Liturgy of the Hours, Vol. II, pp. 1828–1829.
6. Benedict XVI, *Jesus of Nazareth*, (New York: Doubleday, 2007), pp. xxii–xxiii.
7. Saint John Vianney, available at www.catholicbishops.ie.

CHAPTER TWO

1. From *The Rites*, Vol. II (Collegeville, MN: Liturgical, 1990), p. 14.
2. Reverend James Hawker, privately published memoir, pp. 26–27.
3. Archbishop Fulton J. Sheen, *The Priest Is Not His Own* (San Francisco: Ignatius, 2005), pp. 17–18.
4. Sheen, p. 25.
5. Liturgy of the Hours, Vol. III, p. 611.
6. Spoken remarks of Archbishop Francis Xavier Van Thuan.
7. Saint John Chrysostom, *Glimpses of the Fathers*, Claire Russell, ed. (New York: Scepter, 2008), pp. 265–266.
8. Saint John Vianney, available at www.satodayscatholic.com.

CHAPTER THREE

1. Further information about Congressman Father Robert Cornell appears in his privately published memoir *Is There a Priest in the House?* The poem is as quoted by Father John Sherlock, available at www.maiafoundation.blogspot.com.
2. Mother Teresa's acceptance speech is available at www.nobelprize.org.
3. Jeffrey Sachs, *The Economist*, August 14, 1999, p. 17.
4. Saint John Chrysostom, Liturgy of the Hours, Vol. IV, pp. 182–183.
5. Saint John Vianney, available at www.fisheaters.com.

CHAPTER FOUR

1. Saint Anselm, *Liturgy of the Hours*, Vol. I, p. 184.
2. Father Arnold Weber, as quoted in Francis P. Friedl and Rex Reynolds *Extraordinary Lives: Thirty-Four Priests Tell Their Stories* (Notre Dame, Ind.: Ave Maria, 1998), p. 93.
3. *Extraordinary Lives*, pp. 94–95.

4. "Remembering a Man of Prayer: Basil Hume, ten years on," *London Times* online, www.timesonline.co.uk.
5. *London Times* online.
6. *London Times* online.
7. Fulton J. Sheen, *Treasure in Clay* (San Francisco: Ignatius, 1993), pp. 269–270.
8. Saint Norbert, available at www.AmericanCatholic.org.

CHAPTER FIVE

1. Archbishop Timothy M. Dolan, *Priests for the Third Millennium* (Huntington, Ind.: Our Sunday Visitor, 2000), pp. 227–228. I highly recommend this powerful book on priesthood.
2. Pope Benedict XVI, general audience, July 1, 2009.
3. Thomas Kunkel, *Enormous Prayers: A Journey Into the Priesthood* (Boulder, Colo.: Westview, 1999), p. 43.
4. Adapted from the Prayer for Priests from the Archdiocese of Philadelphia.

CHAPTER SIX

1. From homily by Father Mark Szanyi, O.F.M., for the golden jubilee of priesthood of Father Frank Lechiara, pastor of St. Edward the Confessor parish, Palm Beach, Florida.
2. From Cardinal William Levada, "The Homilist Is a Teacher of the Faith," *Origins*, March 6, 2008, pp. 601–607, quoting Cardinal Daneels in *America*, August 27–September 3, 2007, p. 15, and Cardinal Dulles, Letter and Spirit, 2, 2006, 24.
3. Levada, quoting Dulles
4. Levada, *Origins,* March 6, 2008.

CHAPTER SEVEN

1. Adapted from Cardinal Stanislaw Dziwisz, *A Life With Karol* (New York: Doubleday, 2008), pp. 130–136.
2. From the Act of Contrition.

CHAPTER EIGHT

1. From www.hcfm.org.
2. Quoted in Alfred P. McBride, *Images of Mary* (Cincinnati: St. Anthony Messenger Press, 1999), p. 172.
3. From the story of the appearance of Our Lady of Fatima. Available at www.AmericanCatholic.org.

CHAPTER NINE

1. Adapted from Archbishop Timothy M. Dolan, *Priests for the Third Millennium* (Huntington, Ind.: Our Sunday Visitor, 2000), pp. 307–308.
2. Augustine *Confessions,* 6, 11, 20.
3. Paul Loverde, "Bought With a Price: Pornography and the Attack on the Living Temple of God," available at www.catholiccanada.com.

CONCLUSION

1. Saint John Vianney, as quoted in Benedict XVI, Letter Proclaiming a Year for Priests.

2. Whispers in the Loggia, July 18, 2009.

3. Freiherr von Logau Friedrich, available at www.bartleby.com.

4. Pope Benedict XVI, general audience, July 1, 2009.

5. Pope Benedict XVI, general audience, July 1, 2009.

6. Pope Benedict XVI, general audience, July 1, 2009.

7. Liturgy of the Hours, Week III, Saturday morning.

ABOUT THE AUTHOR

ALFRED MCBRIDE, O. PRAEM., holds a diploma in catechetics from Lumen Vitae, Brussels, and a doctorate in religious education from the Catholic University of America, Washington, D.C. He has written many books, including a six-book series on the Bible, four books on the new *Catechism of the Catholic Church,* and *A Short History of the Mass,* and *The Story of the Church.*